Jung in Love

Jung in Love
The *Mysterium* in *Liber Novus*

Lance S. Owens

Monograph Edition

Originally published as a chapter in:

Das Rote Buch – C. G. Jungs Reise zum anderen Pol der Welt
edited by Thomas Arzt
Verlag Königshausen & Neumann, 2015

GNOSIS ARCHIVE BOOKS
LOS ANGELES & SALT LAKE CITY

Monograph edition published by

Gnosis Archive Books
Los Angeles & Salt Lake City

gnosis.org/gab

ISBN-10: 0692578277
ISBN-13: 978-0692578278

I thank Dr. Thomas Arzt for permission to reproduce this
work in a monograph edition. This edition adds illustrations
and minor corrections to the full text originally
published as a chapter in:

Das Rote Buch – C. G. Jungs Reise zum anderen Pol der Welt
Thomas Arzt, editor
Verlag Königshausen & Neumann, 2015

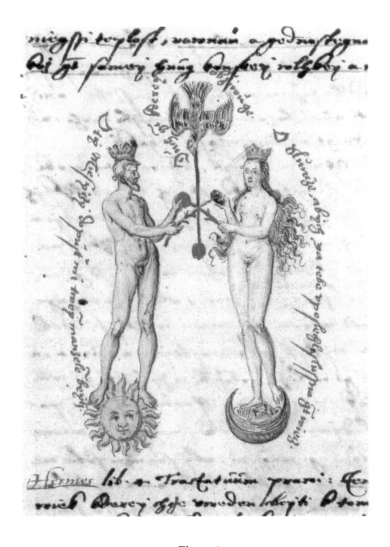

Figure 1
Image from an edition of the *Rosarium Philosophorum* illustrated
by the Czech alchemist Jaroš Griemiller, c. 1578.

Jung in Love:
The *Mysterium* in *Liber Novus*

Lance S. Owens

———

It is my misfortune that I cannot live without the joy of love, of tempestuous, ever-changing love in my life.
  – 1908, *Letter to Sabina Spielrein* [1]

Salome loves me, do I love her? I hear wild music, a tambourine, a sultry moonlit night, the bloody-staring head of the holy one—fear seizes me.
  – 1914, *Liber Novus* [2]

Who exhausts the mystery of love? ... There are those who love men, and those who love the souls of men, and those who love their own soul. Such a one is ΦΙΛΗΜΩΝ, the host of the Gods.
  – 1914, *Liber Novus* [3]

What occurs between the lover and the beloved is the entire fullness of the Godhead. Both are unfathomable riddles to each other. For who understands the Godhead?
  – 1920, *Black Book Journal* [4]

The problem of love seems to me a monster of a mountain which, for all my experience, has always soared to still greater heights whenever I thought I had almost reached the top.
  – 1922, *Letter to Theodor Bovet* [5]

I falter before the task of finding the language which might adequately express the incalculable paradoxes of love.
  – 1961, *Memories, Dreams, Reflections* [6]

———

I.

AT THE CROSSROADS of life, Carl Gustav Jung entered the crucible of conjunction and the mystery of love. It was holy, it was sinful. Hot and cold flowed one into the other. Madness and reason wanted to marry; opposites embraced, intermingled, and recognized their oneness in agonizing pleasure. His heart was filled with wild battle; waves of dark and bright rivers rushed together, crashing each over another.[7] At moments it was pure madness, but he endured. And he returned from the *Mysterium* a man transformed.

Back from the crossroads, he brought a strange record of the journey and called it *Liber Novus*. But he never dared show it to men of his time. He knew they would not understand. Instead, he turned the rest of his life toward molding a hermeneutics for the visions, a method for telling his tale. It became a labor of science, a study of nature, and a confrontation with history at the end of an age. In sum, he called it his *opus psychologicum*.

If this unorthodox journey into the *mysterium* makes Jung a sinner or heretic, then he was. Jung transgressed ethical boundaries in the service of love. He spurned the spirit of his time, listened to the depths, shouldered the burden of his antinomian behavior, and chose his own way. It was the beginning of a New Book. For the rest of his years Jung gave intense consideration to the inner world he had confronted in the midst of love. When in 1942 he began writing a work he thought might become his opus magnum, to be titled *Mysterium Coniunctionis*—"The Mystery of the Conjunction"—love and *Liber Novus* were on his mind.

Jung's relationships with women during these central years of life have been an ethical *casus belli* motivating many damning critiques. Where moral indictments lacked any evidence, assumptions often padded stories about the man's private affairs. But tattled rumors do not tell the tale. And the power and depth of love has figured little in most of the romances about Jung patched together by biographers, dramatists, or psychoanalysts. In consequence, a crux experience of C. G. Jung's life has been miscast or disparaged, and little understood.

And Jung held in hand a private record of his experience, though it was a record entirely unavailable for study until 2009, nearly fifty years after his death. Of course, Jung's intimate annals are ultimately subjective, scribed within the crucible. Nonetheless, they preserve an immediate witness of events and responses to them. It is a clinical record. Dr. Jung kept an historical account of his voyage into vision and love.

A Most Difficult Experiment

Near the end of life, Jung spoke these now familiar words to Aniela Jaffé about the experiences from which *Liber Novus* emerged:

> The years ... when I pursued the inner images, were the most important time of my life. Everything else is to be derived from this. It began at that time, and the later details hardly matter anymore. My entire life consisted in elaborating what had burst forth from the unconscious and flooded me like an enigmatic stream and threatened to break me... Everything later was merely the outer classification, the scientific elaboration, and the integration into life. But the numinous beginning, which contained everything, was then.[8]

While critics might once have held such statements suspect, their truth can no longer be questioned. Publication of *The Red Book: Liber Novus*, and (forthcoming) Jung's Black Book journals,[9] provide primary evidence to the veracity of Jung's words. Based on decades of probing primary sources, Sonu Shamdasani, the editor of both manuscript collections, affirms that *Liber Novus* "is nothing less than the central book in his oeuvre."[10]

These two related records—the *Red Book: Liber Novus* and the "Black Book" journals, from which about half the text of *Liber Novus* is derived—are the bedrock underlying an understanding of the life and work of C. G. Jung. This foundation will, however, be fully comprehended only after a reconsideration of Jung's work in light of "the numinous beginning, which contained everything." That revolutionary reorientation is a generational task. Henceforth any presumption of understanding Jung, absent an appreciation of *Liber Novus* and the mythopoetic experience that engender it, would be in vain.

Jung repeatedly asserted he was a scientist and empiricist, and it might be argued that his later theoretical constructs or conceptual languages should be measured solely on their proven (or disproven) merits, apart from the life experiences of the author. But Jung obscurely disclaimed having theories. Instead, he claimed that his science encircled a most subjective task: the observation of the psyche, the soul. As a clinical investigator, in 1913 Jung fully realized that *one's own psyche* was the only soul offering itself for immediate, direct and intimate observation. Empirically, all else was hearsay, not observation. Jung had only one soul available for observation, and its mystifying terrain was primal soil to the ancient rhizome nurturing his science.

Jung confessed this ultimate subjectivity of his work on several occasions. Speaking in London at the Tavistock Clinic in 1935, he stated: "I consider my contribution to psychology to be my subjective confession. It is my personal psychology, my prejudice that I see psychological facts as I do."[11] He continued, "Never forget that in psychology the *means* by which you judge and observe the psyche is the *psyche* itself. ... In psychology the observer is the observed."[12] At the Eranos Conference in 1946, Jung declared:

> I am profoundly convinced that the "personal equation" has a telling effect upon the results of psychological observation. The tragic thing is that psychology has no self consistent mathematics at its disposal, but only a calculus of subjective prejudices. ... There is no medium for psychology to reflect itself in: it can only portray itself in itself, and describe itself. That, logically, is also the principle of my own method: it is, at bottom, a purely experiential process....[13]

"It can only portray itself in itself, and describe itself." With the *Liber Novus* and Black Book journals at hand, it becomes abundantly clear that the most important observation in Jung's "science" was his direct encounter with his own Soul, itself in itself, describing itself.

In 1913, Jung renounced his prior conceptual framework as "a dead system that I had contrived."[14] He understood that to know the soul, he had to open a direct dialogue with its mystery, itself in itself. It was obtruding into his consciousness, swirling around his dreams, and causing dire visions. Jung had to meet his Soul, whatever soul might be, and wherever she might lead him. Thus began his journal, on 12 November 1913:

> My soul, my soul, where are you? Do you hear me? I speak, I call you—are you there? I have returned, I am here again. I

have shaken the dust of all the lands from my feet, and I have come to you, I am with you. After long years of long wandering, I have come to you again....[15]

Two nights later in the journal record, he addresses his soul:

Who are you, child? My dreams have represented you as a child and as a maiden. *And I found you again only through the soul of the woman.* I am ignorant of your mystery. *Look, I bear a wound that is as yet not healed: my ambition to make an impression.* Forgive me if I speak as in a dream, like a drunkard— are you God?[16]

"And I found you again only through the soul of the woman." At the outset, Jung described his journal as "the book of my most difficult experiment."[17] This record is the essential documentary ledger of his experiment. Despite the ambiguities in voice which the scribal task presented, Jung conducted his experiment with painstaking attention to its record. The first hermeneutic challenge Jung necessarily engaged was bringing his experiences of the soul into the sensuous form of word and image. The venture was to be an empirical observation of the soul, and thus its record was of "scientific" importance. Of course, he allowed that it was anomalous, outside the common line of things. He even struggled with an imaginal feminine voice suggesting it just might be his art.[18] The experiment became a wandering exploration, engaged without map. In itself of itself, it offered the image of a mythic odyssey.[19] In later thoughts, he spoke of it as "a voyage of discovery to the other pole of the world," a place where the "mirror-image begins."[20] And love was a bridge to this realm. In love, Jung found a mirror of his soul.

Jung's observations of his psyche, recorded in the Black Book journals and elaborated in *Liber Novus,* gave pattern to all his subsequent work. In his most self-revelatory account of the experiences—told to a private seminar group in 1925—he admitted that while he used empirical material supplied by his patients in his psychological writing, "the solution of the problem I drew from the inside, from *my* observations of the unconscious processes."[21]

The solution came from his self-observation, his attention to the voice of his psyche. Jung was his own paradigmatic clinical case, and his encounter with psychic reality beginning in 1913 was the empirical key to his dream of a science. The manuscript accounts of Jung's experiences are the primary documentation of his observation of the psyche, itself in itself. Jung's meticulous record—whether it be read simply as a human story, or studied as an anomalous and captivating case history—is astonishing both in the richness of its detail and in the vastness of its hermeneutical implications.

The Hermeneutics of Vision

Having spent about sixteen years recording, calligraphically transcribing and illustrating *Liber Novus*, Jung moved on to creating a conceptual language attuned to the new book's symbolic voice. Jung was seeking his roots, searching for evidences of such experiences in the past. He was developing contexts and concepts for understanding human encounter with the observational fact of the soul: experiences such as he had endured, observations like those reported by a few of his patients.

This is a remarkable fact about Jung's journals and *Liber Novus*: in the vast expanse of his subsequent works, Jung offered a comprehensive, multi-million word hermeneutics directed to these private and unpublished manuscripts. The long sequestered primary documents are Jung's symbolic ledger of a journey into fantasy and vision. It was a venture undertaken accompanied by his feminine soul, within whose realm he confronted the mystery of love. Later in life, Jung spoke about what happened to him cryptically using archaic terms such as *mysterium coniunctionis* and *hierosgamos*. Impelled by his own observations, Jung spent decades hunting this story's tantalizing tradition among the textual legacies of prior times.

Essentially everything Jung wrote after 1916 was in some degree a commentary on his journals and *Liber Novus*. Jung's traditional collected writings, well known before the release of *Liber Novus*, are his supplementary hermeneutics to this veiled primary record.

Based on his "empirical" observations during this intense and transformative experiment, Jung asserted that the psyche was real and had a story to tell. Nonetheless, he realized his immediate record could not then be published: it simply would not be understood. Thus he moved into a secondary interpretive mode. In the years that followed, Jung was contextualizing his hidden work with historical perspectives, while in parallel animating a "scientific" and psychological language adequate to his observations. Sonu Shamdasani explains this next extended period in Jung's work:

[Jung] had completed his descent into the underworld, his "confrontation with the unconscious," and had chosen not to publish *Liber Novus*. Hence he was faced with finding another way of presenting the insights gleaned from his self-experimentation. ... The return to the upper air, by means of comparative historical scholarship, was to be his task and his toil. As Jung later recalled, for fifteen years he studied books to be able to contain what had been revealed to him: "It has taken me virtually forty-five years to distill within the vessel of my scientific work the things I experienced and wrote down at that time."

While *Liber Novus* had been an attempt to present the meaning of the revelation, he now had to come back from the human side—namely, from science. The cost was considerable, and he literally felt that he had paid with his life. ... In an encrypted manner, images and conceptions from *Liber Novus* surfaced, contextualized and amplified. In this regard, one sees that Jung's later works did not follow a straightforwardly linear evolution—first publication did not necessarily coincide with first conception."[22]

Summing the previously published oeuvre to the first source and first conception—that is, to Jung's primary hermeneutics of his experience in *Liber Novus*—requires a conjointly considered reading of both. That is the task in which we now engage. Jung's story cannot be read, nor his clinical history analyzed, without meeting his own carefully made account of the events. Dr. Jung has bequeathed us a bewitching, multileveled reflection on his epochal mythopoetic experience. Apparently, he thought it had something to do with the fundaments of psychology.

The Last Quartet

By 1942 Jung had felt the presage of old age. He was sixty-seven years old and still had work waiting. But a natural conclusion did intuitively loom on the horizon; final statements were coming due. Over prior years he had ranged through the legacy of history, collecting, illuminating and interpreting evidences of human intercourse with a psychic reality he had met. Nonetheless, there were crucial themes in *Liber Novus*—things he privately called his "secret knowledge"—to which he had not been ready to give voice.[23]

The descent of Western civilization into the insanity of a second world war undoubtedly forced Jung's reflections back upon his revelation. *Liber Novus* was begotten in the crucible of the first Great War; prophetic portents of war recorded in his journals during 1913-14 were a decisive factor motivating its composition.[24] Initially, he pondered whether the visions that commenced in 1913 prophesied his own violent psychic disintegration. When the First World War did erupt unexpectedly in August 1914, Jung found objective evidence that his subjective encounter with the voice of the depths had been of more than personal significance: the visions had been prophetic. The outbreak of war impelled Jung to acknowledge that he had received a revelation with epochal implications. In the following months he began writing a first draft of *Liber Novus*. And now, nearly thirty years later, another war returned him to that visionary opus.

The sources and first conceptions underlying the multiplex masterwork that Jung initiated during the early years of World War II have seldom been comprehended. This was Jung's concluding hermeneutic confrontation with *Liber Novus,* and it eventually produced four interrelated works. Together these four books constitute his opus magnum and the consummation of a vocation received thirty years earlier. These works, which I will hereafter refer to as the "last quartet," are: *Psychology of the Transference* (1946), *Aion* (1951), *Answer to Job* (1952), and *Mysterium Coniunctionis* (1955). Recorded in his mature years and all published after a second extraordinary visionary experience, each provides a uniquely focused elaboration and final testament to the "numinous beginning."[25]

It is perhaps characteristic that Jung would end his life's task by circling around a still hidden source from four perspectives, allowing each a voice in turn. However, to understand these late works, one needs to sum them with first conception in *Liber Novus*. In turn, one finds that each offers a finely crafted key to understanding his New Book. The necessity of conjointly reading Jung's later published writings and *Liber Novus* was pronounced by Sonu Shamdasani in his 2009 introduction to the work:

> *Liber Novus* enables a hitherto unsuspected clarification of the most difficult aspects of Jung's *Collected Works*. One is

simply not in a position to comprehend the genesis of Jung's late work, nor to fully understand what he was attempting to achieve, without studying *Liber Novus*. At the same time, the *Collected Works* can in part be considered an indirect commentary on *Liber Novus*. Each mutually explicates the other.[26]

This is particularly true of the books in the last quartet, the late works which I suggest constitute a consciously focused final commentary on *Liber Novus*. Jung began work on this opus in four variations in 1942, with a manuscript which he originally conceived under the title of *Mysterium Coniunctionis*. In the first lines penned on the manuscript, he introduced his overarching theme, "namely, that of the 'mystical marriage.'"[27] What evolved from this first effort to address the mystical marriage was *The Psychology of the Transference*, compose in late 1942 and1943 and published in 1946.

Clothed as a commentary on the patently sexual and symbolic illustrations in the *Rosarium Philosophorum*—a classic sixteenth century alchemical work—and couched in conceptual psychological language, *The Psychology of the Transference* is in bare fact a meditation on the transformative potential of human love. As several readers have intuited over the years, it is a deliberation that touched upon Jung's own experience during the years he was initiated into the imaginal realm of *Liber Novus*.

In 2011, I published the initial installment to this series of essays on the "last quartet" and *Liber Novus*. In that work, "Jung and *Aion*: Time, Vision, and a Wayfaring Man,"[28] I documented how *Aion* was a restatement and development of key themes in *Liber Novus*. In *Aion* Jung speaks his "secret knowledge" and offers his declaration of a coming new age—a core revelation of *Liber Novus*. My intension in that prior publication was to offer a paradigm for placing Jung's last major writings in relationship with their first conception. This chapter is a continuation of that commentary and examines the relationship of the first work in the last quartet, *The Psychology of the Transference*, with the *Mysterium* in *Liber Novus*.

Mysterium

C. G. Jung had experienced a mystery. In late 1913 a voice from the depths awakened. It had something to say, and he gave it focused attention, seeking to comprehend its message. After many sequential nights struggling to find entry into the wonder world of his soul, on 21 December 1913 he consciously crossed the threshold into vision. And there, in an astounding imaginal apparition, he met Salome and Elijah awaiting him. The encounter with Salome and Elijah continued over three evenings, climaxing in a final vision on Christmas. When Jung copied and illustrated the journal account of these events into the Red Book, he titled the episode *Mysterium*. This long section completes "Liber Primus"—the first of the three major sections of *Liber Novus*. In later remarks about his journey, he marked the *Mysterium* as a singularly important event.[29] He recounts the vision's beginning in *Liber Novus*:

> On the night when I considered the essence of the God, I became aware of an image: I lay in a dark depth. An old man stood before me. He looked like one of the old prophets. A black serpent lay at his feet. Some distance away I saw a house with columns. A beautiful maiden steps out of the door. She walks uncertainly and I see that she is blind. The old man waves to me and I follow him to the house at the foot of the sheer wall of rock. The serpent creeps behind us. Darkness reigns inside the house. We are in a high hall with glittering walls. A bright stone the color of water lies in the background. As I look into its reflection, the images of Eve, the tree, and the serpent appear to me. After this I catch sight of Odysseus and his journey on the high seas. Suddenly a door opens on the right, onto a garden full of bright sunshine. We step outside and the old man says to me, "Do you know where you are?"
>
> I: "I am a stranger here and everything seems strange to me, anxious as in a dream. Who are you?"
>
> E: "I am Elijah and this is my daughter Salome."[30]

The visionary meeting with Elijah and Salome continued intensifying over three nights and forms one of the longer encounters in *Liber Novus* (and here "vision" is the precise word Jung used to describe the experience). Jung called these visions his "transformation."[31]

About a decade later Jung privately penned a reflection on the figures encountered: "They are certainly not intended allegories; they have not been consciously contrived to depict experience in either veiled or even fantastic terms. Rather, they appeared as visions."[32] At the conclusion of the first night's vision, Jung exclaims to Salome and Elijah, "You are the symbol of the most extreme contradiction." Elijah corrects him: "We are real and not symbols."

Elijah explains that he and his daughter, his "Wisdom," have been one from the beginning. Salome declares her love for Jung, and explains that she is his sister; their mother is Mary. At the denouement of the vision, which occurred on Christmas 1913, Jung is Christed—he suffers the last hour on Golgotha. Here, *Liber Novus:*

Salome says, "Mary was the mother of Christ, do you understand?"

I: "I see that a terrible and incomprehensible power forces me to imitate the Lord in his final torment. But how can I presume to call Mary my mother?"

Salome: "You are Christ."

I stand with outstretched arms like someone crucified, my body taut and horribly entwined by the serpent: "You, Salome, say that I am Christ?"

It is as if I stood alone on a high mountain with stiff outstretched arms. The serpent squeezes my body in its terrible coils and the blood streams from my body, spilling down the mountainside. Salome bends down to my feet and wraps her black hair round them. She lies thus for a long time. Then she cries, "I see light!" Truly, she sees, her eyes are open. The serpent falls from my body and lies languidly on the ground. I stride over it and kneel at the feet of the prophet, whose form shines like a flame.

Elijah: "Your work is fulfilled here. Other things will come. Seek untiringly, and above all write exactly what you see."

Salome looks in rapture at the light that streams from the prophet. Elijah transforms into a huge flame of white light. The serpent wraps itself around her foot, as if paralyzed. Salome kneels before the light in wonderstruck devotion. Tears fall from my eyes, and I hurry out into the night, like one who has no part in the glory of the mystery. My feet do not touch the ground of this earth, and it is as if I were melting into air.[33]

Jung wrote privately that no other event in *Liber Novus* shared the quality of these visions.[34] This experience marked a doorway of mystery. Jung passed through. At the end of the *Mysterium*, Elijah gave an explicit mandate: "Other things will come. Seek untiringly, and above all write exactly what you see." Jung complied.

Enantiodromia of the Life-type

Into the draft text of *Liber Novus*, Jung inserted several extended (and heavily reworked) passages on the meanings of *Mysterium*. The passages were apparently composed as additions to concluding paragraphs of "Liber Primus," but were subsequently omitted from the transcription in the calligraphic volume.

Jung meditated on Salome and Elijah in these draft additions, interpreting the figures as fateful representatives of two opposite elements within him, which were demanding attention. Elijah embodied thoughts and ideas, or "forethinking" (*das Vordenken*). Salome was a messenger of both his unmet "desire" (*die Lust*) and the transformation of multifold desiring into love.[35] Jung was struggling with this mystery of love. He wrote, addressing his readers:

> The God holds love in his right, forethinking in his left. Love is on our favorable side, forethinking on the unfavorable. This should recommend love to you, insofar as you are a part of this world, and especially if you are a thinker.[36]

Jung was a thinker, and his desiring (*die Lust*) was blind. But the *Mysterium* visions worked a change on him. He continued in the draft text:

> Here the wonder happened that my previously blind desire [*die Lust*] became sighted. My desiring was blind, and it was love. Since my strongest willing willed self-sacrifice, my desiring changed, it went into a higher principle, which in God is one with forethinking [*das Vordenken*]. Love is sighted, but desire is blind. Desiring always wants what is closest, and feels through the multiplicity, going from one to another, without a goal, just seeking and never fulfilled. Love wants what is furthest, the best and the fulfilling....[37]

In closing words to this draft commentary, Jung states that the visionary events of the *Mysterium* foreshadowed what awaited him:

> The Mysterium showed me the things which lay before me and had to be fulfilled. But I did not know how and when. But that image of the sighted Salome, who knelt in rapture before the white flame, was a strong feeling that came to the side of my will and led me through everything that came after. What happened was my wandering with myself, through whose suffering I had to earn what served for the completion of the Mysterium I had seen.[38]

In the 1920s, Jung wrote a private reflection on *Mysterium*.[39] There he again considers the union of Eros and Logos—feminine and masculine principles—as prefigured in the meeting with Elijah and Salome. Jung's dominant function had been thinking and reason, "Logos." But, he explained, "In this, my case, ... Logos has blinded and subjugated Eros."[40] He continues:

> But if this is the case, then the necessity will also arise to free Eros from the clutch of Logos, so that the former will regain vision. Therefore Salome turns to me, because Eros is in need of help, and because I have apparently been enabled to behold this image for precisely this reason.

In the draft of *Liber Novus*, he had earlier written,

> I rejected my feeling, but I had rejected part of life. Then my feeling became a poisonous plant, and when it awakened, it was sensuality instead of pleasure, the lowest and commonest form of pleasure. ... Salome is the image of this pleasure, that suffers pain, since it was shut out for too long. It then became apparent that Salome, i.e., my pleasure [desiring, *die Lust*], was my soul.[41]

Eros—*his eros*, appearing as Salome—was blind, and needed help. The sightless and unmet aspect of his human nature required healing: Eros awaited relationship with Logos.[42] In the *Mysterium*, Jung was caught between two worlds. The unifying and healing act mandated that he descend into earthy facts of flesh. He continued:

> The acceptance of the undeveloped is therefore like a sin, like a false step, a degeneration, a descent to a deeper level; in

actual fact, however, it is a greater deed than remaining in an ordered condition at the expense of the other side of our being, which is thus at the mercy of decay.[43]

A sin, a degeneration: and yet it was the healing deed. Two years before his death, Jung described his task as climbing down and reaching out his hand "to the little clod of earth that I am."[44] A few months earlier, Jung wrote to R. F. C. Hull, explaining that without first meeting the "Mysterium Iniquitatis"—all those things that fascinated Freud and made up the shadow and the chaos of man's chthonic desires—"I could not have found an access to the 'Mysterium Coniunctionis'."[45]

Jung prefaced his 1920s analysis of *Mysterium* with a short and cryptic title line: "Enantiodromia of the life-type." Those few words well summarize what had happened to him. The *Mysterium* was the beginning of a transformational "enantiodromia" in his life. In later writings, Jung frequently employed the term *enantiodromia* to mean the "reversal of an extreme into its opposite."[46]

In his 1942 Eranos lecture, "The Spirit of Mercurius"— composed around the time he began writing about the *Mysterium*— he gave another veiled commentary on this experience. The lecture, like much in Jung's published writings, reflected conceptions and experiences rising up from *Liber Novus*. Jung begins by discussing the traditional view of Christ as Logos—the light from light—and the later millennial enantiodromia that befell the Christian age, the moment when alchemy turned from the otherworldly light of Logos back towards the dark mystery of matter. He explained the turn:

> Consciousness is no longer confined within a sacred temenos of otherworldly, eschatological images.[47] It was helped to break free by a force that did not stream down from above— like the *lumen de lumine*—but came up with tremendous pressure from below and increased in strength as consciousness detached itself from the darkness and climbed into the light.[48] In accordance with the principle of compensation which runs through the whole of nature, every psychic development, whether individual or collective, possesses an optimum which, when exceeded, produces an enantiodromia, that is, turns into its opposite.[49]

On Christmas night of 1913, Jung faced an individual enantiodromia: Logos turned and met Eros ascending. Soul and woman awaited. It was transformative; it was the doorway into a mystery of conjunction.

II.

Whatever unseen psychic currents finally pushed Jung to begin writing his commentary on the *Mysterium*, two works he read during 1942 did evidently fertilize his thoughts and influence its commencement. The first text—and this is the one he mentions twelve years later in the foreword to *Mysterium Coniunctionis*—was an essay received from Karl Kerényi on the "Aegean Festival" in Part II of Goethe's *Faust*. Jung decoded this scene as Goethe's imaginative confrontation with the mystical marriage. Both his *Mysterium* and the many years he had spent hunting records of such experiences in history unquestionably influenced his reading of Goethe's poetic vision. In the 1954 foreword, Jung begins by explaining that he "first got the idea" to write about the *Mysterium Coniunctionis* more than ten years before, from Kerényi's essay on Goethe's "Aegean Festival." Then he adds: "The literary prototype of this festival is *The Chymical Wedding* of Christian Rosencreutz, itself a product of the traditional hierosgamos symbolism of alchemy."[50] Thus, Jung locates Goethe's mystical marriage within a traditional lineage of imaginative encounters with the sacred wedding—which is, incidentally, where Jung situated his own.

Around the time he received Kerényi's essay, Jung also was reading another and much older text about the mystical marriage: the *Aurora Consurgens*, an alchemical work attributed to Thomas Aquinas. Marie-Louise von Franz was then preparing an edition for publication, and had asked Jung to write a preface. Sonu Shamdasani suggests the latter event was a first impetus to Jung's volume; he quotes a 1951 letter from Jung's secretary, Marie-Jeanne Schmid, to Cary Baynes detailing what transpired after Jung began studying some of von Franz's labors on *Aurora Consurgens*: "he became so fascinated with her material, he asked her if she would mind if he wrote a book on it, and the 'preface' swelled to eight hundred pages."[51]

The Psychology of the Transference

On the first draft page of the budding book, Jung penned his title: *Mysterium Coniunctionis.* The manuscript starts by declaring that a leitmotif runs throughout "our *mystical tractus,*" the *Aurora Consurgens.*[52] The theme, Jung explains, is "namely, that of the 'mystical marriage.'"[53] What follows in manuscript is the introductory page to the published edition of *The Psychology of the Transference*—the first phase of the last quartet, written mostly during late-1942 and 1943, and completed in the fall of 1945.[54]

I cannot give here an in-depth commentary on *Psychology of the Transference.* My intention is, instead, to suggest that the book already contains its own analysis and commentary on the relational events that opened up *Liber Novus.* Until Jung's source in *Liber Novus* is figured, what he was doing with this study will neither be understood nor usefully commented upon.

In *Psychology of the Transference* Jung employed a sixteenth-century alchemical text to provide context and cover for what is fundamentally a statement about his own observations of the psyche many years earlier. When Jung began writing about the mystery of the conjunction in 1942, he was deliberating upon his *Mysterium*—events recounted both in his journals and in *Liber Novus.* In itself and of itself, Jung's journey into the *Mysterium* is the empirical bedrock underlying the commentary presented in *Psychology of the Transference.*

To understand that development, however, one must both examine how he retold his tale in this later commentary, and then reflect it back upon source and first conception. I will begin with a review of the later commentary, and then, in the next sections of this chapter, examine the original conception in the threshold events that opened *Liber Novus.*

Words for a Mystery

The voice Jung selected in his initial effort to write about the mystery of the conjunction took a distinctly "scientific" and psychological tenor. He approached the *mysterium* through the empirical doorway of a phenomenon widely discussed in prior analytic literature: the transference. The "transference" is a classic affair supposedly observed in psychoanalytic therapy, wherein images and fantasies originating from the patient's unconscious are projected onto the analyst and into the therapeutic relationship.

Jung begins by explaining the difference between his assessment of transference phenomena and the position enunciated by Freud. Freud insisted the transference was an essential component of his psychoanalysis, and that the material projected upon the analyst by the patient would almost invariable replicate some prior incestuous familial bond, typically one with mother or father. Through re-emergence in the transference, repressed and unconscious rudiments of such infantile relationships—Freud's theoretical source for neurosis—could be analyzed.

Jung differed. In his experience, transference was neither a necessary nor inevitable component in every analytical relationship. Nor were transference phenomena limited to the consulting room; they are encountered in human affiliations more generally.[55] And while projections of incestuous mother or father relationships upon a therapeutic liaison did undeniably occur, sometimes the transference evoked symbolic images rooted in deeper substrata of the unconscious, actualities that did not originate from repression of earlier life experience. These primal symbolic contents, or "archetypes," were natural constituents of human nature, akin to instincts.

The *Coniunctio*

This brief preface brought him to the central assertion of his study. The most complex and challenging primordial archetype sometimes arising through a transference is the *coniunctio*, the image of the mystic marriage: "The *coniunctio* is an *a priori* image that occupies a prominent place in the history of man's mental development." (§355)[56]

Jung offers historical examples where symbolic images of the *coniunctio* are evidenced, noting their ubiquity in alchemical texts, and in sources flowing forward from both pagan and Christian mysticism. "These psychic experiences and the traces they have left behind in tradition explain much that would otherwise be totally unintelligible in the strange world of alchemy and its secret language." (§355)

Furthermore, he alleges that they also explain a fact witnessed in medical psychology (speaking of his own), where the archetype of the *coniunctio* is observed materializing as the imaginative expression of a key unconscious process. "The alchemical image of the *coniunctio* ... plays the same role in the exploration of the darkness of the psyche as it played in the investigation of the riddle of matter." (§355)

Where does one witness the appearance of this primordial and symbolic image of the *coniunctio*? "Practical analysis has shown that unconscious contents are invariably projected at first upon concrete persons and situations." (§357) Relationship is the magic mirror wherein one meets this mystery. Of course, magic mirrors are tricky; the projection affects both parties, and may produce a bond between them:

> This bond is often of such intensity that we could almost speak of a "combination." When two chemical substances combine, both are altered. This is precisely what happens in the transference. (§358)

> ...The patient, by bringing an activated unconscious content to bear upon the doctor, constellates the corresponding unconscious material in him, owing to the inductive effect which always emanates from projections in greater or lesser degree. Doctor and patient thus find themselves in a relationship founded on mutual unconsciousness. (§364)

Throughout the book, Jung uses an apotropaic distinction between "doctor" and "patient." But of course, with discretion, he is ultimately speaking of a transformative relationship between two human beings. Under exceptional circumstances the hierarchy implied by terms such as patient and doctor could utterly disintegrate, to the effect that each would become both things in relation to the other. This had happened to Jung.

Induction of the *coniunctio* triggers myriad erotic and instinctual energies, "forms of instinctive *concupiscentia*."[57] The human instinctual and imaginative inheritance is, in Jung's view, a spectrum ranging from concrete sexual impulses at one extreme, to "unreal" and "spiritual" symbolic contents (like the mystical marriage) at the other.[58] Upon this spectral continuum, physical and imaginal facts mirror, merge and refract in a most confusing way. He explains:

> Not only are there different instincts which cannot forcibly be reduced to one another, there are also different levels on which they move. In view of this far from simple situation, it

is small wonder that the transference—also an instinctive pro-cess, in part—is very difficult to interpret and evaluate. The instincts and their specific fantasy-contents are partly con-crete, partly symbolical (i.e., "unreal"), sometimes one, some-times the other, and they have the same paradoxical character when they are projected.

In any particular case it is often almost impossible to say what is "spirit" and what is "instinct." Together they form an im-penetrable mass, a veritable magma sprung from the depths of primeval chaos. (§362-3)

Whenever this "magma sprung from the depths of primeval chaos" erupts symbolically into an analytic relationship (or any intimate human relationship),

...every trace of routine then proves to be a blind alley. Con-sequently the higher psychotherapy is a most exacting busi-ness and sometimes it sets tasks which challenge not only our understanding or our sympathy, but the whole man. (§367)

Jung lays this basic groundwork in the first twenty or so pages of his introduction to *Psychology of the Transference*—pages that com-prise the first four of its ten sections. In the remainder of the intro-duction, he tracks the story of the *coniunctio* back into the alchemical quest for a mercurial wedding of masculine and feminine natures, and the stark schism of spirit and flesh that haunted Chris-tianity.

To speak cogently about this mystery, however, Jung faced the hermeneutic challenge of gathering language apt to a lived and still living experience. How could he revivify seemingly dead words—old words like *coniunctio oppositorum*, *hierosgamos*, and *mysterium coni-unctionis*—with a modern imagination? He pronounced his task:

Eternal truth needs a human language that alters with the spir-it of the times. The primordial images undergo ceaseless transformation and yet remain ever the same, but only in a new form can they be understood anew. Always they require a new interpretation....

What is that about "new wine in old bottles"? Where are the answers to the spiritual needs and troubles of a new epoch? And where the knowledge to deal with the psychological

problems raised by the development of modern consciousness? (§395-6)

A Symbolic Tongue

After that introduction, Jung moves into the meat of his book. To
find language adequate for the task, Jung chose a series of ten alchemical woodcut images and aphorisms from the *Rosarium Philosophorum*—the "Rosary of the Philosophers," a classic alchemical
treatise first printed in 1550.[59] The images Jung selected to convey
the intricacies of transference have puzzled many readers over the
years—they seem a bizarre semantics for psychotherapy. The pictures pursue a manifestly sexual path into esoteric meaning. Each
woodcut illustrates a phase in the relationship between a royal cou-
ple, a king and a queen. In an initial image, king and queen extend
and join hands. Then follow pictures sequentially showing the cou-
ple disrobing, submerging together in bath, and then uniting in sexual intercourse. Next, the postcoital pair suffers death, fused
together as a bizarre hermaphrodite. Thereafter the woodcuts progressively illustrate their revivification and final resurrection as a
royal androgyne.

Jung weaves plentiful threads of psychological meaning into this
symbolic alchemical treatise. Early on, he introduces his key concepts of anima and animus, the indwelling contrasexual psychic
companions of man and woman. This leitmotif animates all that follows. Jung points out that the eros of relationship between a man
and woman involves unseen interior companions and their mysterious desiring. As he explained in the introduction, dark denizens and
symbolic contents of the psyche are first met projected outward onto another person. A man finds his anima first in the face of a real
woman, unaware that what he sees mirrored there has reality within
him. A woman does the same, finding reflected back from man the
insubstantial interior animus—a masculine fact residing in woman.
When psychic and somatic actors are all correspondingly roused, the
relationship becomes a mesmerizing and muddling four-way face-
off.[60] The pair in relationship appears outwardly to be simply a man
and woman—or in alchemical vocabulary, the *adept* and *soror mystica* (mystical sister). But each has another unseen and living agent
acting within. The anima within the man and the animus within the
woman are equally real, and they too wish liaison.

Figure 2
Page from the Czech edition of the *Rosarium Philosophorum* illustrated by
Jaroš Griemiller, c. 1578. Jung reproduced woodcut images from the original 1550
Frankfurt edition of *Rosarium Philosophorum* in "The Psychology of the Transference."

Jung's hermeneutic approach to his material is a masterfully contrived articulation of the *coniunctio* as a primordial image casting its spell upon human intercourse. The goal of this higher *coniunctio* is not simply an instinctual coupling of man and woman. In and through eros, men and women meet their own soul images projected upon a partner. The royal wedding involves creative union with this interior and otherwise unconscious domain evoked by the projection.

> There is in the *coniunctio* a union of two figures, one representing the daytime principle, i.e., lucid consciousness, the other a nocturnal light, the unconscious. Because the latter cannot be seen directly, it is always projected.... For this reason it is felt to be something alien to us, and we suspect it of belonging to the particular person with whom we have emotional ties. In addition a man's unconscious has a feminine character; it hides in the feminine side of him which he naturally does not see in himself but in the woman who fascinates him. ... The personal side of it is a fact, but not the main fact. The main fact is the *subjective experience* of the situation—in other words, it is a mistake to believe that one's personal dealings with one's partner play the most important part. Quite the reverse: the most important part falls to the man's dealings with the anima and the woman's dealings with the animus. (§469)

A personal relationship—a physical fact—does exist. But it is not on this immediate level that the *coniunctio* comes into focus:

> Nor does the *coniunctio* take place with the personal partner; it is a royal game played out between the active, masculine side of the woman (the animus) and the passive, feminine side of the man (the anima). Although the two figures are always tempting the ego to identify itself with them, a real understanding even on the personal level is possible only if the identification is refused. (§469)

Relationship with a partner opens the Janus gate to mysteries of the soul. By arousing the anima, and mirroring her vitality, a woman might open for a man the hidden passage between inner and outer realms. This can presage a path leading toward individuation, the union of lucid consciousness and nocturnal light. The ultimate goal of psychological work is—Jung asserted—conscious realization of psychic reality and its nocturnal light. A first phase in that work is accomplished by meeting the indwelling soul image projected outward upon one's partner:

> The supreme aim of the *opus psychologicum* is conscious realization, and the first step is to make oneself conscious of contents that have hitherto been projected. This endeavour gradually leads to knowledge of one's partner and to self-knowledge, and so to the distinction between what one really is and what is projected into one, or what one imagines oneself to be. Meanwhile, one is so taken up with one's own efforts that one is hardly conscious of the extent to which "nature" acts not only as a driving-force but as a helper—in other words, how much instinct insists that the higher level of consciousness be attained. This urge to a higher and more comprehensive consciousness ... if it is to fulfil its purpose, needs all parts of the whole, including those that are projected into a "You." (§471)

The primordial image of the *coniunctio* finds a helper in instinctual nature, itself in itself. Erotic, relational energies can urge conscious realization, if one can face the reality that is projected into a "You," and discern its primal source. Jung claims that in alchemy the *coniunctio* is "a symbol of the supreme and ultimate union ... bringing the work to its final consummation and binding the opposites by love, for 'love is stronger than death.'"[61] Likewise in his psychology, the *coniunctio* is a consummate binding of opposites: night with day, inner with outer, above with below, sense with nonsense, consciousness with unconsciousness. Love could be mercurial agent of the *coniunctio*.

Passions of Flesh and Spirit

In the final pages of *Psychology of the Transference*, Jung draws a summary contrast between Freud's viewpoint and his own. At the end of the nineteenth century Freud had brought sexuality within the scope of psychological discussion; Jung acknowledges the importance of that singular effort. Human relationships involve instinctual sexuality; this is an undeniable fact haunting us from within. But there was another haunting instinct: the longing for creative intercourse with the nocturnal light of the Soul. Jung had experienced it. This primordial human instinct was evidenced in the ancient story of the *hierosgamos* or *coniunctio*, the "holy wedding." It was also empirically evidenced in psychotherapy, where the *coniunctio* archetype emerged again in the "transference neurosis."[62]

By elucidating this instinct for the sacred wedding, Jung was finishing what Freud had started. Though utterly repugnant to Freud, Jung affirmed there are two sides to instinctual nature: we experience physical desires, and we suffer passions of spirit. In higher human relationships, both sometimes mingled. We live in two worlds. As he explained in *Liber Novus*:

> If you look into yourselves, you will see ... the nearby as far-off and infinite, since the world of the inner is as infinite as the world of the outer. Just as you become a part of the manifold essence of the world through your bodies, so you become a part of the manifold essence of the inner world through your soul. This inner world is truly infinite, in no way poorer than the outer one. Man lives in two worlds.[63]

In the outer world, Jung faced the irrefutable facts of flesh. In the inner, he met a primordial soul awaiting relationship. These two realities touched each other: Psychic reality was in relationship with its materiality, and matter met spirit. In the transference phenomenon, Jung recognized what he claimed to be objective evidence of this *coniunctio* archetype pressing into consciousness; it was a primordial image also historically evidenced in ancient and sacred dreams of the mystical wedding. The consummation of this wedding—the union of two realities indwelling human nature—was individuation, a becoming whole. Facts of flesh and facts of soul met in the *mysterium*.

I find it impossible to read *Psychology of the Transference* without hearing it as a deeply considered commentary on Jung's own life and subjective observations of the soul. He implies as much in the book's concluding comments:

> We are moving here in a region of individual and unique happenings that have no parallel. ... Its inmost essence is the uniqueness of a life individually lived—which nobody can grasp from outside, but which, on the contrary, holds the individual in its grip. (§538)

Jung had been gripped by the image of the *coniunctio* in all its complexity at the end of 1913. It was his doorway and path:

> The Mysterium showed me the things which lay before me and had to be fulfilled. … What happened was my wandering with myself, through whose suffering I had to earn what served for the completion of the Mysterium I had seen.[64]

In 1945, he concluded this first attempted commentary on the mystery of conjunction by stating:

> The transference phenomenon is without doubt one of the most important syndromes in the process of individuation; its wealth of meanings goes far beyond mere personal likes and dislikes. By virtue of its collective contents and symbols it transcends the individual personality and extends into the social sphere, reminding us of those higher human relationships which are so painfully absent in our present social order, or rather disorder. (§539)

III.

When Jung began writing about the mystical marriage in 1942, he was consciously composing commentary upon a *mysterium* he had lived. Judging by the first approach he took, Jung regarded human relationship as a key to the experience—or, at very least, it had been *his key. The Psychology of the Transference* might be read as his book about the key that turned the lock that opened the door that revealed the mystery. The initial step in his *opus psychologicum* was becoming conscious of psychic contents projected onto a partner.

By 1913 and the age of thirty-eight, Carl Jung had experienced his projections upon women. All evidence suggests that Jung possessed an intense sensitivity to the feminine psyche, and he realized it. Women responded to him. One might say Jung had a powerful "anima complex"—but that analysis evokes a vocabulary which developed only much later, and as a result of his self-observation. Before 1914, Jung had no clear sense of what the anima might be. Lacking fully developed concepts of anima, projection and transference, the word "love" was perhaps the only sufficient term he had for his experience. But what was love? What did *it* want? Why did *he* want *it*?

To comprehend the events that brought Jung to the doorway of *Liber Novus*, one must reflect on his struggle with love. Love opened the New Book. I know it is a delicate subject, and one that has been much abused in prior treatments. Nonetheless, a century after the events, I believe enough primary documentation exists to allow one at least to sketch a story of Jung in love.

Real Women

Four women met Jung in love during the decade that led to the New Book. The most important was certainly Emma Rauschenbach.[65] Jung first briefly saw Emma when she was just seventeen, and was immediately smitten. He knew that she must become his wife. After a courtship of about three years, Emma and Carl wed in February 1903; she was then twenty and he was twenty-seven years old. Emma was the sustaining love of Jung's life. His polygamous nature caused her suffering, but despite the problems Jung brought into their marriage, he was never alienated from her. And she stuck it out with him for fifty years.[66]

After forty years of marriage, I think it is significant that Jung dedicated *The Psychology of the Transference* to Emma: "To My Wife." In the book he made mature confessions, and drew conclusions, about things he had lived. Emma had witnessed it all. Toward the book's end he said,

> The process of psychological differentiation is no light work; ... a radical understanding of this kind is impossible without a human partner. A general and merely academic "insight into one's mistakes" is ineffectual, for then the mistakes are not really seen at all, only the idea of them. But they show up acutely when a human relationship brings them to the fore and when they are noticed by the other person as well as by oneself. Then and then only can they really be felt and their true nature recognized. Similarly, confessions made to one's secret self generally have little or no effect, whereas confessions made to another are much more promising.[67]

Maybe those last words were underlined for Emma—they should have been. When they married, Jung was inexperienced, introverted, and puzzled about love. He had a long path to pace with psychological differentiation. Over the first decade following marriage, three other women powerfully touched his life; from these relationships radical understandings resulted. He differentiated his feelings. Nevertheless, it sometimes must have been chaos for those nearest him. One of the women he loved during these years—Toni Wolff—remained a part of Emma and Carl's lives until her death in 1953. It was a strange situation. Maybe it taught the man something about love.

Sabina Spielrein

Until 1980, the name of Sabina Spielrein (1885-1942) was known mostly through a few footnotes in the writings of Freud and Jung, and by scattered mention in the Freud-Jung Letters. All that changed in 1977 when a cache of her private papers—including intimate diaries, and her correspondence with both Jung and Freud—was found in Geneva. Some of the documents were first published in 1980 by Aldo Carotenuto, accompanied by his historical and interpretive commentary. Over the next twenty years, more material from the cache came to light. These primary documents have now generated a voluminous secondary literature, including John Kerr's 1993 study, *A Most Dangerous Method.* The story of Spielrein, Jung and Freud has been imaginatively (and inaccurately) dramatized in theatrical and cinematic productions. It is a beguiling story, and one proven to trigger plentiful projections.

Sabina Spielrein was the daughter of a wealthy Russian Jewish family. At the age of nineteen she was sent to Switzerland for psychiatric treatment, and then for enrollment in medical school. An intelligent and well-educated young woman, in adolescent years Sabina developed increasingly bizarre, compulsive and aggressive manners of "acting out." In one of her extreme states, on the night of 19 August 1904 she was carried into the Burghölzli hospital, and entered under the care of twenty-nine year old Dr. C. G. Jung. At the time, Jung was barely four years out of medical school. He had no personal experience with psychoanalysis—of course, hardly anyone did. Psychoanalysis was a new methodology advocated by a physician on the fringe of European psychiatry. But Jung had read Dr. Sigmund Freud's *The Interpretation of Dreams* (1900) and taken note. So, Dr. Jung elected to test Dr. Freud's talking cure with this young and challenging hysteric patient.

Over the next months Sabina slowly disclosed to Jung a history of physical abuse at the hand of her father. This trauma seemingly led to masochistic sexual fixations, and aggressive, socially repellent behaviors. Or, at least, analyzing the problem with those factors in view did have healing effect. Talking to Jung—sorting out a way of seeing and speaking about the deeper forces that had possessed her—helped Sabina. After about five months in hospital under treatment with Jung, she was mostly cured of her behavioral malady. The following June, she entered medical school at the University of Zürich, now with the intention of becoming a psychiatrist and psychoanalyst. She excelled, received her medical degree in early 1911, and was thereafter accepted by Freud as the second woman member of his Vienna Psychoanalytical Society. Dr. Sabina Spielrein was one of the small number of women—and by far the youngest—to publish in the early psychoanalytical literature.

During her years in Zürich, Sabina kept private journals about the relationship with Jung and saved copies of their letters. In these she wrote passionately, expressively, and sometimes analytically. Her diaries expose the experience and insights of an intuitive young woman, deeply afflicted by love for Carl Jung. No longer a patient after 1905, Sabina had become Jung's close friend. Within a year or so, Jung was struggling with something like love for Sabina. The letters and journals picture an intimate intellectual and psychological relationship developing between the two. By 1908, they were both in the soup, and both analyzing the madness of what was happening to them.

Sabina was possessed by the image that she must bear Jung a son, who would be named Siegfried. The image of this son born from their union possessed Sabina's imagination. The child seemed to be a heroic and indispensable result of their union. Of course, both of them knew this was crazy. But it *was so*—it was a myth of transformative love, and Sabina felt it must happen in fact, in flesh. Both doctor-psychoanalyst and doctor-psychoanalyst-in-training were struggling to understand this "veritable magma sprung from the depths of primeval chaos."[68] Neither of them had answers. Why the heroic child? Where does this fantasy of Siegfried come from?

Where does it point? How do such things so powerfully possess us? Love was working its terrible magic on them both.

By 1909, rumors of an affair involving young Dr. Jung were apparently whispered around Zürich. Under mistaken impression that Sabina was the source of the rumor and that a scandal was brewing, Jung briefly broke off contact with her. However, several months later they were again keeping company. They remained on affectionate terms through early 1911, when Sabina completed her doctorate and abandoned Zürich. Though they did not see each other again after 1911, letters between the two up through 1919 are preserved in Sabina's treasure cache of memories.

Boundaries of Love

Was this a sexual affair? Regardless of evidence to the contrary, the usual explicit or implicit assumption is that it must have been. In the extensive analytic literature published in the last decades about Spielrein and Jung, the commentary most often focuses ethically and conceptually on Jung's supposed "boundary violations" within a therapeutic relationship, or on his failure to properly handle the transference and counter-transference issues uncovered by the affair. Other critiques have bluntly cast the situation as the sexual exploitation of a vulnerable young woman by her psychiatrist, a man abusing his position of trust and authority. Despite such assumptions or assertions, there is no evidence that the interaction of Spielrein and Jung included sexual intercourse. More to the point, the preponderance of evidence—including their many private statements—strongly argues that it did not.

Zvi Lothane, a Freudian psychoanalyst and scholar of psychoanalytic history—who, moreover, harbors no bias towards excusing Jung—makes the most robust and well-supported case against a sexual relationship between the pair.[69] Examining all the published documents, and adding new evidence he has found in Sabina's cache, Lothane convincingly contends that the relationship between Jung and Spielrein was tender and loving, but not sexually consummated. Based on my own reading of available sources over the last twenty years, I concur. Dr. Lothane summarizes his conclusions:

> People tend to believe as dictated by their own emotions, projections, and transferences. ... Our judgment should really be guided by what the protagonists never tired of asserting

themselves: that there was no sex. In the final analysis the question is whether we believe their testimony or not. I choose to believe them, and not out of prudery, but because in those days people saw premarital sexual relations, especially as applies to Spielrein, differently than we do today; moreover, because unconsummated sexual desire was even more poignant and more romantic than consummated sex. However, the sexual myth dies hard, providing sensational material for a number of theatrical productions and a plethora of articles in the popular press and professional journals.[70]

So, what were the boundaries of this affair? In the first years, an intellectual and emotional rapport clearly developed between the pair. Jung spoke with Sabina openly as a friend and mentor; she labored to understand who this man was, and why she so loved him. After about two years, a reciprocal bond had formed; Jung was suffering love. They engaged physical expressions of their affection; Sabina described these in her journals and letters as their "poetry." She portrays Jung kissing her fingers and lips, staring into her eyes as tears came to his own, and embracing. But Jung refused to "give her a child," which is to say, engage in sexual intercourse. That was his limit, and he would not cross it. For Sabina, it was torture—she struggled, but accepted it would be just so.

Sabina had a very candid relationship with her mother, who evidently was quite experienced in the ways of men and love. At the end of 1908, she wrote her mother, giving an update (one of many such letters) on the situation with Jung:

> That I love him is as firmly determined as that he loves me. He is for me a father and I am a mother for him, or, more precisely, the woman who has acted as the first substitute for the mother (his mother came down with hysteria when he was two years old); ... Twice in a row he became so emotional in my presence that tears just rolled down his face! Then he starts reproaching himself endlessly for his feelings, for example, that I am something sacred for him, that he is ready to beg for forgiveness, etc. ... This conversation took place almost two weeks ago and we both felt literally tormented, unable to utter a word, etc. ... We stood still in the most tender poetry. ... Will I ever in my life forgive him for what he had

concocted with me … will he ever forgive me for what I have done to him! The difference is that I know that for him scientific activity is above all else in life and that he will be able to bear everything for the sake of science. The question is only how my intellect is going to relate to this whole story and the trouble is that the intellect does not know how to relate. … *So far we have remained at the level of poetry that is not dangerous, and we shall remain at that level, perhaps until the time I will become a doctor, unless circumstances will change.* [Emphasis in the original][71]

In that letter, and in many other places in her writings, it is clear that the "poetry" Sabina made with Jung was a tender, often ecstatic, but constrained physical intimacy. It was love poetry, intensified by longings denied— "and the trouble is that the intellect does not know how to relate."

Did it stay that way, or did circumstances change? In Sabina's diary entry of 11 September 1910—just a few months before graduating from medical school, and leaving both Jung and Zürich —she mused again upon her dream of bearing Jung's son. Sabina saw in reality how totally impossible it was, how it would ruin her chance of finding another love and destroy her scientific and professional ambitions:

> With a baby I would be accepted nowhere. And that would be in the best of cases; what if I did not even get pregnant? Then our pure friendship would be destroyed by the intimate relationship, and our friendship is what is so terribly dear to me.[72]

Mark those words: Sabina realized that even if they were to finally have sexual relations, she might not get pregnant. And having taken that step, "our pure friendship would be destroyed by the intimate relationship…." I find no ambiguity in those words, privately scribed in her diary soon before she left Zürich.

Was this unconsummated love poignant and compelling, as Zvi Lothane suggests? Traditions reaching back at least to the troubadours suggested it could be.[73] But to know empirically, one would need to enter the experiment, itself in itself. For six years, Spielrein and Jung evidently probed the poignancy, pain and psychological power of sexually unrequited love.

CONIVNCTIO SIVE
Coitus.

① Luna durch meyn vmbgeben/vnd susse mynne/
Wirstu schön/ starck/vnd gewaltig als ich byn.
① Sol/ du bist vber alle liecht zu erkennen/
So bedarsstu doch mein als der han der hennen.

ARISLEVS IN VISIONE.

Coniunge ergo filium tuum Gabricum dile=
ctiorem tibi in omnibus filijs tuis cum sua sorore
Beya

Figure 3
Woodcut image from the 1550 Frankfurt edition of *Rosarium Philosophorum*,
reproduced by Jung as Figure 5 in "The Psychology of the Transference."

Two Speakers

In the diary, Sabina recounts her experience with Jung's "anima"—though of course that term was not yet coined. She sensed that she was in relationship with a feminine image inside of him. Early in the liaison, she asks herself, 'What really is this abominable thing that is love?'[74] She recognizes the projective nature of love: "What do we love in the other? Our own ideal."[75] Sabina sees the contrasexual images at work, and addresses Jung:

> Still you must be aware that my 'unconscious' does not want
> to have anything to do with what your 'unconscious' rejects.
> ... The complexity of the situation makes me adopt the un-
> natural role of the man and you the feminine role.[76]

In *Psychology of the Transference*, Jung points out the "royal game played out between the active, masculine side of the woman (the animus) and the passive, feminine side of the man (the anima)."[77] Sabina and Jung were playing the royal game without a rulebook.

Jung gave Sabina his journal to read, explaining that she and his wife were the only people to have seen it.[78] Sabina reflects on Jung's love for Helene Preiswerk, his cousin, the young medium who was the subject of his dissertation: "you held the young woman in greater esteem than anybody else, and [you said] that you thought she was destined for you." But Jung found out "the young imp" was scheming. He says to Sabina, "She too seemed to me like a goddess, but in the end she turned out to be just a flighty girl." With irritation, Sabina infers that Jung is comparing his prior love for Helene with what he is now seeing in her.[79] He was projecting a goddess image, and then questioning the nature of the woman who conjured it up in him.

In an undated journal extract—probably written in 1906 or 1907—Sabina addresses a long meditation on love to Jung. She titled it, "The theory of transformation and its corollaries." By way of preface, she pens an enigmatic contemplation on "Two speakers." Sabina has intuited two opposing voices in Jung: one voice is nurtured by passion (*die Leidenschaft*), the other is controlled by a logical spirit (*der Geist*):

> Of the two speakers, one reaches the summit of his art only
> when he gives himself up to passion [*die Leidenschaft*]: it is
> passion that warms his brain into life, irrigates it and forces

his spirit [*der Geist*] to show its strength. The other ... is at the peak of his power when he resists the impetuosity of his emotions and, as it were, makes fun of them: it is only then that his spirit comes right out of its hiding place, a logical spirit, derisive, playful but nonetheless terrible.[80]

Seven years later Jung would recognize an unresolved rift in his nature between passion and spirit: he then called the pair *die Lust* and *das Vordenken*, "Desiring" and "Forethinking," or Eros and Logos. In his *Mysterium* this duality appeared as Salome and Elijah; soon thereafter it manifests again in *Liber Novus* personified as "The Red One" and "Ammonius."

Sabina is trying to understand the transformative power of unrequited love. She writes,

Considering its nature, sexual feeling does not need the transformation instinct, but it is present nonetheless; yet the transformation instinct needs the sexual feeling, the latter being a necessary component of the first; otherwise how would the combinations survive?[81]

This same insight is echoed nearly forty years later in *Psychology of the Transference*. Jung reflects that instinct is a helper to the transformation: "One is hardly conscious of the extent to which 'nature' acts not only as a driving-force but as a helper—in other words, how much instinct insists that the higher level of consciousness be attained."

The diaries and letters preserve only fragments of a private dialogue that matured from 1904 to 1911. When Jung and Spielrein parted ways, they bid farewell as dear friends. Between 1916 and 1919 Spielrein and Jung again corresponded, but now addressed each other more formally. At the time of these late letters, Jung had been through the fire; he had experienced and written *Liber Novus*. In one of his final notes, Jung openly expressed to Sabina how important their love had been to him. The letter is dated 1 Sept 1919:

The love of S [Spielrein] for J [Jung] made the latter aware of something he had previously only vaguely suspected, namely of a power in the unconscious which shapes our destiny, a power which later led him to things of the greatest importance. The relationship had to be 'sublimated' because otherwise it would have led to delusion and madness (the concretization of the unconscious). Sometimes we must be unworthy to live at all.[82]

Those words may have brought closure for Jung, but it remains uncertain that they did so for Sabina. The love of S and J had to be "sublimated." In the psychoanalytic language they both spoke fluently, sublimation meant the diversion or transformation of an instinctual energy to higher or more acceptable forms. Jung had sublimated their sexual desiring to "things of greatest importance." Sabina had introduced him to a power in the unconscious, but Jung intuited it could not then be concretized through a physical relationship. That would have meant madness, at least for him.

Three years after they separated, Jung finally and directly visioned the interior fact that had so passionately and so obscurely animated his affairs. To this almost forgotten Soul he said: *"And I found you again only through the soul of the woman."*

Maria Moltzer

Was Jung philandering? Were there women besides Spielrein in Jung's life during the years before he entered the alembic that brewed up his *Liber Novus*? Each reader will cast a different story from the meager documentation. Many women loved Jung, and he surely projected his own sacred images into some of those personal or analytical liaisons. If that is love, then he loved. Around the end of 1908, Sabina wrote her mother:

> Look, how many female patients have been to see him and, without fail, each one of them would fall in love with him but he could only act as a physician because he did not love in return! But you know how desperately he struggled with his feelings![83]

His apparent refusal to engage a sexual relationship with Spielrein does, however, suggest something about Jung's caution with his much-analyzed "sexual complex." He wrote Freud in February 1910:

> At present I am sitting so precariously on the fence between the Dionysian and the Apollinian [sic] that I wonder whether it might not be worthwhile to reintroduce a few of the older cultural stupidities such as the monasteries. That is, I really

don't know which is the lesser evil. … The ethical problem of sexual freedom really is enormous and worth the sweat of all noble souls. But 2000 years of Christianity have to be replaced by something equivalent.[84]

The dominant spirit in Jung—call it his "noble soul" and Apollonian nature, his terrible *Geist*, or his subjugating *Logos*—seemed basically inclined toward *explaining* his "sexual complex" rather than fully submitting to its alluring Dionysian madness. Maybe the monastery was where he belonged. Four years after that letter to Freud, Jung would end up in the Syrian Desert with a Christian ascetic, contemplating the light of the Logos. As related in *Liber Novus*, his visit with this noble anchorite concluded on a distinctly devilish note.[85]

There was at least one woman with whom Jung developed another intricate relationship around this time. Tall, thin, blond-haired and blue-eyed, Maria Moltzer was a Dutch nurse working at the Burghölzli hospital. Under Jung's tutelage, she had become an analyst. An heiress to the Dutch *Bols* distilling and liquor fortune, she was personally opposed to alcohol due to the social problems it wrought. While in Zürich, Moltzer maintained a generally frugal and abstemious lifestyle, and concealed her family's wealth.

Responding to Jung's claim that he—unlike Freud—had at least been analyzed, in December 1912 Freud wrote about Jung and Moltzer to Sándor Ferenczi:

He is behaving like a florid fool and the brutal fellow that he is. The master who analyzed him could only have been Fraulein Molzer [sic] and he is so foolish as to be proud of this work of a woman with whom he is having an affair. She is probably the one who got him worked up immediately upon his return to Zürich. [86]

Sonu Shamdasani has documented Moltzer's previously unrecognized contributions to the analytical community in Zürich and her influence on the development of Jung's psychological typology. He also has published several of her previously unknown papers, talks originally presented in 1916 and 1917 to the analytical group surrounding Jung in Zürich.[87] That she was a trusted analyst and assistant to Jung from 1912 onward is unquestionable.[88] Details about her personal relationship with Jung are, however, not so well documented. Surviving letters between them have not been disclosed.

According to Jung's then developing criteria, to become an analyst one first had to be analyzed. Moltzer probably underwent her analysis with Jung. If one believes Freud, she may thereafter have in turn analyzed Dr. Jung. Or perhaps the analytic process was naturally concurrent—something not entirely unlike what had informally happened with Spielrein over the prior years. Jung was attracted to Maria. In conversation with Aniela Jaffé in 1957, Jung describes Maria Moltzer as a "terrific creature" who had an "enormous transference" on him. He recognized a powerful image within himself emerging in their association, which he began then understanding as the anima.[89] Was there sex? According to Jung's statements in *Psychology of the Transference*, higher human relationships are aided by sexual instincts, even if necessarily sublimated. Moltzer and Jung did develop an "enormous transference" relationship.

Moltzer was one of the limited group around Jung who had read his draft manuscript of *Liber Novus*. She was in frequent company with him throughout the period from late-1913 to 1914 when he underwent the initial experiences, and undoubtedly she heard some accounts of his imaginative venture directly from him. In Moltzer's talks delivered during 1916 and 1917, one senses that she was addressing herself primarily to Jung; they were in dialogue. Her subjects touch upon themes evoked by *Liber Novus*.[90] Among the people attending the presentations there were a few others who had read Jung's manuscript, and they would have recognized Moltzer's points of reference.

Highly intuitive, Moltzer developed her own hermeneutic approach to analysis and the imaginative, creative instincts residing within the unconscious. It was Moltzer who introduced the "intuitive function" into Jung's psychological typology. In her available writings, she emphasizes both the personal and the collective aesthetic, artistic and religious implications of intercourse with the psyche—things she also saw exemplified in Jung's creative work on his Red Book. This *was* art.[91] At the same time, Moltzer was crafting her own "bible" in image and word, in parallel to Jung's labor with the Red Book. But Jung found her artistic focus irritating and, moreover, ultimately antagonistic to an understanding of his visionary experiences.[92] What she saw as art, he understood as nature.[93] In

1918 they had a break. Moltzer resigned from the Psychological Club and thereafter permanently departed Zürich.

The relationship with Maria Moltzer cast its spell on Jung; she challenged his hermeneutics of imaginative experience, and influenced the conceptual development of his psychology. However, another person entered Jung's life around the time he met Maria. Love for this other woman seems to have utterly changed him.

Toni Wolff

Memories, Dreams, Reflections—the classic 1961 biographical memoir constructed by Aniela Jaffé—makes little mention of Jung's relationships with women. Jaffé's rendition of Jung's "Confrontation with the Unconscious"—the period when he began the Red Book—may leave readers with the impression that he retreated into an imaginative cloister: a monk alone with pen, parchment and a horde of ghostly guests.[94] But he was not entirely alone. Speaking from experience, Jung explained in *Psychology of the Transference* that unconscious contents are first met in relationship with a partner. The events recorded in *Liber Novus* were mediated through relationship to both outer and inner facts. His principal outer partner was apparently Toni Wolff.

Toni Wolff is not mentioned in *Memories, Dreams, Reflections*—a book inaccurately understood over the last half-century as Jung's personally scribed account.[95] Those closest to Jung knew Toni had played a mysterious and crucial role in his life. That she remained a companion, along with his wife Emma, throughout subsequent decades was no secret. Jaffé's failure to even note Toni's name in her book pained many people who knew their story. Few readers understood, however, that the failure was not a matter of Jung's choice. In his 1957 interviews with Jaffé, he talked candidly about the relationship with Wolff. Those comments, along with a wealth of other things Jung said in the conversations, were excluded from the heavily edited memoir.

Jaffé's original transcript of her interviews with Jung—known as the "Protocols"—is available in the Library of Congress; more related material is archived in Zürich.[96] Jung's remarks in the Protocols about the relationship with Wolff provide important perspectives on the origins of *Liber Novus*, and I will review some of them here. For a general overview of Jung's relationship with Wolff, Barbara Hannah's 1976 biography remains essential reading; unlike other biographers, Hannah knew all the parties very well for several decades and was one of first people to publish an account of the role Wolff played in Jung's life.[97]

Toni Wolff was born in 1888, the eldest daughter of an old and distinguished Zürich family. She was close to her father; after he died suddenly in 1909, Toni fell into a deep depression. In 1910, her mother took her to Dr. Jung for treatment; Wolff was twenty-two and Jung thirty-five years old at the time of their meeting. Jung's analytic intervention helped her. He related to Jaffé that at the beginning of analysis Toni had an eruption of the wildest fantasies, some of incredible, cosmic, nature. Her fantasies paralleled Jung's line of thought, but—he said—he was so preoccupied with his own material that he could then scarcely take on hers as well. Nonetheless, she made enough progress in analysis that by September 1911 Jung invited Wolff to join the Zürich contingent attending the Weimar psychoanalytic conference—a group which included Maria Moltzer and Emma Jung (though invited, Spielrein did not attend). In a letter to Freud, Jung introduced the young conference attendee: "a new discovery of mine, Frl. Antonia Wolff, a remarkable intellect with an excellent feeling for religion and philosophy...."[98]

Jung told Jaffé that he recalled the exact moment when the "problem" of Toni was put to him. He had completed her analysis, and discharged her from his care (around the end of 1911, or early 1912). It was the correct thing to do, he said, in spite of his feeling of being involved with her. Then about a year after terminating the analysis, he dreamt he was with Toni in the Alps. They were together in a valley of rocks, near a rock wall. Suddenly Jung heard the soft voices of the elves singing inside the mountain. Toni was on the point of sinking into the mountain, pulled by the elves. Jung thought, this cannot be allowed. In the dream, Jung tore Toni away from the elves and rock face. At that moment, he told Jaffé, he knew it was unavoidable that he reestablish their relationship. Soon thereafter, he wrote to Wolff.[99] This seems to have been around the beginning of 1913.

There were other dreams during this period which he thought concerned Toni. In one, he met a woman who was from the waist down all stone, but alive from the waist up. Jung realized that he had given the woman an injection into the spinal fluid, so that she had turned to stone. He describes the dream as "horrible." About the same time, he had a frightening physical experience: he swam out into Lake Zürich and then got a severe cramp. Thinking he might drown, at that moment he made a vow: if he were able to survive and make it back to shore, he would "give in" and contact Toni. Jung interpreted this event as indicating his own life was in danger if he did not act to reestablish the relationship.

Shortly after Christmas 1912 another dream came; this one is recounted by Jaffé in *Memories, Dreams, Reflections*. Jung dreamt that a white dove had flown in the window, alighted on the table, and then turned into a little girl eight years old.[100] A year later, in November 1913, Jung wrote in his journal that it was this dream which "made him decide to embark on a relationship with a woman he had met three years earlier," Toni Wolff.[101]

Intriguingly, in the introduction to *Psychology of the Transference* Jung chose to recount a remarkably similar dream that had been brought to him by a patient. In her dream, a six-month-old child had appeared. Jung comments:

> It is immediately apparent that the child is something special, i.e., a child hero or divine child. ... The square table is the quaternity, the classical basis of the "special" child.... The precise age of the child made me ask the dreamer to look in her notes to see what had happened in the unconscious six months earlier.[102]

Following his instructions, she looked back in her notes, retrospectively calculating the time of the child's birth, and then figuring the time of the child's conception. At each past moment, the patient found a portentous event recorded. Perhaps Jung gave the same type of analysis to his dream: eight years before the "little girl of eight years" appeared in this December 1912 dream, Jung met Spielrein. That event birthed a mounting analytic confrontation with powers emanating from his mysterious, unmet anima.

Hearing Her Voice

From Jung's account to Jaffé, it is clear he sensed an ominous need to engage with Wolff. But why that need was knocking, Jung did not know. At the same time, he had a complex relationship in progress with Moltzer. And there was his wife, Emma, whom he loved.

The man was in difficult straits. In *Psychology of the Transference* Jung described what awaited him:

> The supreme aim of the *opus psychologicum* is conscious realization, and the first step is to make oneself conscious of contents that have hitherto been projected. This endeavour gradually leads to knowledge of one's partner and to self-knowledge, and so to the distinction between what one really is and what is projected into one, or what one imagines oneself to be.[103]

So, when did Jung finally take that first step? He had met something sacred mirroring in several women—Emma, Sabina, Maria, Toni, and perhaps others. When did he meet the source in himself? The step seems to have come in November 1913, shortly after he began writing in his journal the words that started *Liber Novus*. In 1925, he described the event:

> I said to myself, "What is this I am doing, it certainly is not science, what is it?" Then a voice said to me, "That is art." This made the strangest sort of impression upon me, because it was not in any sense my impression that what I was writing was art. Then I came to this, "Perhaps my unconscious is forming a personality that is not I, but which is insisting on coming through to expression."[104]

Jung identifies the interior voice that said, "this is art" as Moltzer's voice. His unconscious was forming an independent personality and seeking its voice. To start, it took hers. He explained to Jaffé, "through her [Moltzer] the anima dawned on me." Barbara Hannah perceptively remarked, based on things Jung told her:

> As far as I know, this was the first time Jung became aware of the phenomenon of projection, and of withdrawing it. ... Jung was still unaware of the figure of the anima within himself, so she projected herself into this woman, as it were, and used her voice. Jung was thus able to recognize that something he had so far seen in this woman really belonged to an inner figure in himself.[105]

During his 1925 seminar, Jung recounted that this was the prelude to his progressively active dialogue with the soul, or—using the old Latin term—the "anima."[106]

Woman and Soul

Every past biography of Jung plays a riff on his relationship with Wolff, begun around 1913. Most of it is pure improvisation, hung off a few factual keynotes. Imaginative scenes have been fabricated freehand by some biographers.[107] But none of these accounts had access to Jung's own journal record, nor to *Liber Novus*. Now that we do have his primary accounts, what changes?

About three-quarters of the text in *Liber Novus* is based on the visionary fantasies erupting between November 1913 and April 1914, augmented by commentary added in the year thereafter. This was Jung's initiatory event—though, of course, it was followed by several more years of journal records, and his further imaginative layering of imagery into the calligraphic Red Book, all of which continued through the 1920s. But it was during this concentrated initial period that Jung initially engaged a paradoxical relationship with both his soul and a real woman.

Before constructing further commentaries on Jung's relationship with Wolff, one must recognize that Jung did write his own in his commentary contemplating the mystical marriage. The task awaiting students of Jung now is conjoining Jung's primary account of his experience, recorded in the journals and *Liber Novus,* with his mature reflection on these complex relational events—particular as they are enunciated in his last quartet of works. Jung was probably speaking about facts met in relationship with Toni Wolff when he wrote the following words in *Psychology of the Transference*:

> The unrelated human being lacks wholeness, for he can achieve wholeness only through the soul, and the soul cannot exist without its other side, which is always found in a "You." Wholeness is a combination of I and You, and these show themselves to be parts of a transcendent unity whose nature can only be grasped symbolically....

> Hence wholeness is the product of an intrapsychic process which depends essentially on the relation of one individual to another. Relationship paves the way for individuation and makes it possible, but is itself no proof of wholeness. The projection upon the feminine partner contains the anima and sometimes the self.[108]

In her insightful 2014 study, the Brazilian analyst Maria Helena R. Mandacarú Guerra argues that a singular Ariadne's thread weaves throughout the Red Book: Jung's love drama with Toni Wolff.[109] This assertion is alluring, and it may pilot some readers who would be otherwise lost in the labyrinth of *Liber Novus*. Jung did say, "The soul cannot exist without its other side, which is always found in a 'You.'" However, as absolutely essential as human relationship was to Jung, he recognized that this liaison was running in concert with images emerging from the depths. Relationship paved a way, but wholeness resulted from an intra-psychic process worked through conjunction with outward relationship:

> Individuation has two principal aspects: in the first place it is an internal and subjective process of integration, and in the second it is an equally indispensable process of objective relationship. Neither can exist without the other, although sometimes the one and sometimes the other predominates.[110]

Of course, these are Jung's later conclusions, written three decades after the events. In 1914 he was in confusion. The conceptual map and guardrail of his later psychological terminology did not then exist for him—that came only in reflection on his experiences. Anima, transference, and counter-transference were *not* words he was employing to understand what was happening to him. That was the language of his science, and he had fallen from its theoretical path:

> All kinds of things lead me far away from my scientific endeavor, which I thought I had subscribed to firmly. I wanted to serve humanity through it, and now, my soul, you lead me to these new things. Yes, it is the in-between world, the pathless, the manifold-dazzling.[111]

Jung was meeting imaginative experience; he was observing the soul itself in itself, as it found a voice and began speaking for itself. Elijah and Salome were not symbols, but real. Though such declarations are difficult to grasp in extraverted terms, by the beginning of 1914 Jung was in an intense dialogic relationship with his mythopoetic imagination and feminine soul. In the *Mysterium*, Salome petitioned his love, and prophesied: "You will love me." Love was the word Dr. Jung was confronting: the image and fact and experience of love. Love was the word he wrote in *Liber Novus*—the word appears around three hundred times in the text. And I suspect one will count that word "love" being repeated just as often in his journals during this period. The drama of love involved both a human relationship and a relationship of interior union. It was a *coniunctio*. Love demanded confrontation with and acceptance of his subjugated Eros. Jung was meeting the awful division in himself. He wrote in *Liber Novus*,

> I rejected my feeling, but I had rejected part of life. Then my feeling became a poisonous plant, and when it awakened, it was sensuality instead of pleasure, the lowest and commonest form of pleasure. ... Salome is the image of his pleasure, that suffers pain, since it was shut out for too long. It then became apparent that Salome, i.e., my pleasure, was my soul.[112]

> On the right is my thinking, on the left is my feeling. I enter the space of my feeling which was previously unknown to me, and see with astonishment the difference between my two rooms.[113]

His encounter with Salome and Elijah in the *Mysterium* opened a new understanding of these two rooms. He called it his "transformation." Two voices spoke, and he pondered their conjunction: Eros and Logos; *die Lust* and *das Vordenken*—or, as Sabina named the voices eight years earlier, *die Leidenschaft* and *der Geist*. Or was it the opposing psychological functions of feeling and thinking that he met?[114] Words, words: what words could he use to interpret this fact of self and soul? It was all bubbling together in a broth of love.

Transgression

At this threshold, Jung understood that he must sacrifice his one-sided heroic spirit to the passions and feelings of flesh. He had to face, as it were, the issue of incarnation: he had to live his animal.[115] I can here only sketch the account in *Liber Novus*, and offer a few glimpses of events evolving. One must read these sections of the book carefully to catch what is happening.

On the evening of 26 December 1913, the night after conclusion of the *Mysterium*—the beginning point for "Liber Secundus" in *Liber Novus*—Jung stands watch alone on his solitary tower. He sees a red figure in the distance approaching. It is the Red One: the fiery emissary of *die Lust* and devilish joy, a neglected half of himself. He meets his personal devil, and while they converse, the Red One takes a more human cast. As the vision fades, Jung calls out to the Red One: "Could you be joy? I see you as through a cloud. Your image fades. Let me take your hand, beloved, who are you, who are you?"[116]

On a rainy night next up in his wanderings, he finds shelter within a scholar's castle in the forest. As he tosses and turns alone in bed, a maiden enters the room. She has been locked away in the scholar's castle, and seeks freedom through his recognition. He struggles against the absurdity of his fantastic situation—a puerile "farmer's daughter" romance—but lastly grants the maiden her reality: "How beautiful and worthy of adoration is the expression of your soul in your eyes. Happy and enviable is the man who will free you." She asks, "Do you love me?" He replies, "By God, I love you—but—unfortunately I am already married." She bids him farewell: "So—you see: even banal reality is a redeemer. I thank you, dear friend, and I bring you greetings from Salome."[117]

The visionary path soon leads into the desert, where he encounters Ammonius, a third-century Christian anchorite reading the Gospel of John day after day, and contemplating the solitary light of the Logos. They converse about the mystery of words. Ammonius' solitude resonates with a factor in Jung's own nature: "The solitary lives in endless desert full of awesome beauty. He looks at the whole and at inner meaning. He loathes manifold diversity if it is near him. He looks at it from afar in its totality."[118]

And then, just a few evenings later, the Red One and Ammonius reappear in another imaginative scene, each now having been corrupted by the other—an enantiodromia of the life-type that took both to ruin. Jung perceives the two figures as images of his own "Degenerate Ideals," abstract modes he is now discarding. They have become for him simply "The Remains of Earlier Temples."[119] Jung was greening, sprouting leaf and new life.

A few weeks later, after spending many sequential nights engaged with the beauty, darkness and threatening chaos of his inner world, Jung deliberates with his Soul on the rapidly evolving situation:

I: "How holy, how sinful, how everything hot and cold flows into one another! Madness and reason want to be married, the lamb and the wolf graze peacefully side by side. It is all yes and no. The opposites embrace each other, see eye to eye, and intermingle. They recognize their oneness in agonizing pleasure. My heart is filled with wild battle. The waves of dark and bright rivers rush together, one crashing over the other. I have never experienced this before. ... I am rigid with tension. Loving reaches up to Heaven and resisting reaches just as high. They are entwined and will not let go of each other, since the excessive tension seems to indicate the ultimate and highest possibility of feeling."

Soul: "You express yourself emotionally and philosophically. You know that one can say all this much more simply. For example, one can say that you have fallen in love all the way from the worm up to Tristan and Isolde.

I: "Yes, I know, but nonetheless—"

Soul: "Religion is still tormenting you, it seems? How many shields do you still need? Much better to say it straight out."[120]

Jung had fallen in love, from the earthy worm all the way up to Tristan and Isolde in a sacred grotto called Amour. "How holy, how sinful... Madness and reason want to be married." And he was conflicted: this love—both inwardly and in its outer action—involved a transgression of moral certitudes, his lingering "religion."

The relationship between Jung and Wolff was obviously deepening during these winter month of 1914. Biographers offer variant particulars, supported by scattered recollections. Jung's record in *Liber Novus* tells only about his wanderings in the vastness of the inner world he was discovering. In the Protocols, he explained to Jaffé that he couldn't talk with anyone other than Toni Wolff about the inner experiences, and she was in the same mess and without orientation. He described the situation as "absolutely awful."

If—or when—Carl Jung and Toni Wolff consummated a physical relationship, it probably was a few months after the above passages were penned. Perhaps "it" happened, as some have supposed, on their journey together to Ravenna in early spring of 1914. Whatever the private details, a sin was being forced by love. Two years later, Jung wrote in the final section of *Liber Novus:*

I had to remain true to love, and, devoted to it voluntarily, I suffer the dismembering and thus attain bonding with the great mother, that is, the stellar nature, liberation from bondage to men and things. If I am bound to men and things, I can neither go on with my life to its destination nor can I arrive at my very own and deepest nature. ... Only fidelity to love and voluntary devotion to love enable this binding and mixing to be dissolved and lead back to me that part of my self that secretly lay with men and things. Only thus does the light of the star grow, only thus do I arrive at my stellar nature, at my truest and innermost self, that simply and singly is.

It is difficult to remain true to love since love stands above all sins. He who wants to remain true to love must also overcome sin. Nothing occurs more readily than failing to recognize that one is committing a sin. Overcoming sin for the sake of remaining true to love is difficult, so difficult that my feet hesitated to advance. [121]

Esther Harding chronicled Jung's comments—spoken to her a few years later, in 1922—about transgressing moral boundaries:

Thus, vice too, if entered into sincerely as a means of finding and expressing the Self, is not vice, for the fearless honesty cuts that out. But when we are bound by an artificial barrier, or by laws and moralities that have entered into us, then we are prevented from finding, or even from seeing that there is a real barrier of the Self outside this artificial barrier....

If we are conscious, morality no longer exists. If we are not conscious, we are still slaves, and we are accursed if we obey not the law. He [Jung] said that if we belong to the secret church, then we belong, and we need not worry about it, but can go our own way.... [122]

A Lover of the Soul

Thus it was that love was an agent and a doorway into the *mysterium*; it aroused powers and images of unification. But the images presented in his visions or fantasies were not indicative solely of union with a human partner. Jung understood that he was differentiating and conjoining fragments of himself, powers that had been seen before only in projection, inner facts cast outward into women, men and things. Now these actualities implored integration within him.

The mystery that had captivated Dr. Jung's interest over many prior years—perhaps reaching back to childhood—was the cryptic psychic background of consciousness. As clinician and physician, he had witnessed psychic forces chaotically possessing and commanding human behavior. He now urgently needed to fathom *his* personal relationship with the primordial psychic background of conscious life. Through love he was delving into longings within himself. Jung sought liberation from the illusory *maya* of his unconscious projections, because "only thus do I arrive at my stellar nature, at my truest and innermost self, that simply and singly is." He explained in *Psychology of the Transference*, "This urge to a higher and more comprehensive consciousness ... if it is to fulfill its purpose, needs all parts of the whole, including those that are projected into a 'You.'"[123] In love, Jung was struggling to find the interior origin of powers looming outwardly in relationship, forces that were seeking conjunction within his own being. In this task, a magician came to his aid.

Jung first met the magician Philemon—his ghostly guide to the wonder world of the soul—around the end of January 1914, during the same few months that were critical between Jung and Toni Wolff. The relationship with Philemon would transform through several layers of complexity over the next years. Jaffé quotes Jung saying that Philemon introduced an attitude of psychic objectivity, a "superior insight" into his experiences:

> It was he who taught me psychic objectivity, the reality of the psyche. Through him the distinction was clarified between myself and the object of my thought. He confronted me in an objective manner, and I understood that there is something in me which can say things that I do not know and do not intend, things which may even be directed against me.

> Psychologically, Philemon represented superior insight. He was a mysterious figure to me. At times he seemed to me quite real, as if he were a living personality. I went walking up and down the garden with him, and to me he was what the Indians call a guru. [124]

The commentary in *Liber Novus*, probably written in draft around the beginning of 1915, describes Philemon much more intimately:

Now I know your final mystery: you are a lover. You have succeeded in uniting what has been sundered, that is, binding together the Above and Below. ... Who exhausts the mystery of love?

Under which mask, Oh ΦΙΛΗΜΩΝ [Philemon], are you hiding? You did not strike me as a lover. But my eyes were opened, and I saw that you are a lover of your soul, who anxiously and jealously guards its treasure. There are those who love men, and those who love the souls of men, and those who love their own soul. Such a one is ΦΙΛΗΜΩΝ, the host of the Gods.

...Are you still a man, ΦΙΛΗΜΩΝ, or is one not a man until one is a lover of one's own soul?[125]

Jung envisioned that he—like his master Philemon—was becoming a lover of his own soul. Such love was the higher nature, the greater power, and the transformative potential of human love: this love constellated the *mysterium coniunctionis*.

Philemon, Simon Magus and Helena

While reciting this strange history, I find myself again struck by how peculiar it all sounds. Who could believe such a tale? How should a reader understand this experience? Of course, Jung well understood the problem: he was living it, and his sense of isolation was immense. Nevertheless, he intuited that his observations of the soul, itself in itself, could not be entirely unique in history. So he enquired: Who else had shared this journey? Where were the records of other wayfaring men who strode into the soul world, and found a mystery of love? He recognized marks of the event in Nietzsche, though it heralded not union, but a solitary madness.[126] Goethe, in part two of *Faust*, seemed to have imaginatively ventured into the terrain Jung now traveled (Goethe is mentioned several times in the manuscripts of *Liber Novus*).[127]

By the time Jung finished the draft of *Liber Novus* in 1915, he was at work hunting through human history for records of others who had walked this visionary road of mystery. And it was not just accounts of visions that he sought—those were quite common enough. He was searching for records of a specific experience of love and the relational image of the mystical marriage, interior events that opened the door to the "secret church" and led to "the stellar nature, liberation from bondage to men and things." Philemon played a role in this search for historical roots.[128]

Jung stated repeatedly to Barbara Hannah, that "the *first* historical parallels he found to his experience were in the Gnostic texts," that is, those recorded by the ancient Christian writer Hippolytus (170—235 CE), in his work *Elenchos*.[129] Jung did not speak to Hannah of finding parallel concepts or ideas, but of finding parallel experiences. So, what did he find in the ancient accounts of Hippolytus that paralleled his own strange intercourse with the soul? I have written at length elsewhere about Jung's reading of Hippolytus and early Gnostic texts, historical explorations Jung undertook during 1915. Here I give a summary of that discussion.[130]

In the ultimate vision recounted in *Liber Novus*—and recorded in his journal on 1 June 1916—Jung is walking in the garden with Philemon. Christ appears there to them both. Philemon addresses Christ as "my master, my beloved, my brother!" Christ sees Philemon, but recognizes him as Simon Magus—a principal figure in the ancient Gnostic tradition. Philemon explains to Christ that once he was indeed Simon Magus, but now: "Simon and Helena have become Philemon and Baucis and so we are the hosts of the Gods."[131]

Simon Magus, "the Magician," is the first historical figure named in the earliest accounts of the Gnosis. The dates of his life remain unclear; most ancient reports place Simon in the first century of the Christian era. Second century critics generally identified Simon Magus as the father of Gnostic "heresy." Writing in the late-second century, the orthodox apologist Irenaeus called him "the Samaritan Simon, from whom all the heresies took their origin."[132] The most extensive primary source on Simon Magus is Hippolytus; writing in the early-third century, Hippolytus recounts both Simon's history and quotes from texts attributed to him.

Stories about Simon's life emphasize that he had a consort named Helena, or Helen. Later opponents asserted that Helena was just a whore who Simon picked up in the Phoenician port of Tyre and then freed. Simon told the story differently, adding a mythopoetic dimension to their relationship. He proclaimed that through the woman Helena he had recognized a deific feminine power. Helena was a manifestation of the divine *Sophia* (Wisdom); by her mediation, Simon had met the primal *Epinoia*. This Greek term, *Epinoia* (imperfectly translated with the words "thought" or "conception"), appears often in Gnostic mythologies as the title for the primal feminine emanation manifest within the primordial mystery of divinity.[133]

Simon says of her: "Wisdom was the first Conception (or Thought) of my Mind, the Mother of All, by whom in the beginning I conceived in my Mind the making of the Angels and Archangels."[134] Using gender symbolically, he explained that the *masculine* Mind, or Logos, was in primordial relationship with a *feminine* syzygy, which Simon named *Epinoia*—the primal first Thought of the divine Mind. G. R. S. Mead commented upon this story in 1900, explicitly noting its psychological nature:

> The Logos and his Thought, the World-soul, were symbolized as the Sun (Simon) and Moon (Selēnē, Helen); …Helen was the human soul fallen into matter and Simon the mind which brings about her redemption.[135]

When Jung read this text in 1915— and also read Mead's commentary above—he saw images of a lover of the soul: Simon *was* Philemon. Simon's relationship with Helena paralleled Jung's passage in love with both a woman and a godlike feminine image. This may have been the *first* historical account he found that reflected his own experience.

Recall Jung's *Mysterium*, in which he met Elijah and Salome. Upon first seeing Salome, he was shocked by her presence with the prophet, and questioned, "Was she not vain greed and criminal lust?" Salome nonetheless declared her love for him and wished to become his bride.[136] Jung recognized he loved Salome.[137] In his draft emendations to *Liber Novus*, Jung pondered the relationship of the masculine mind (described as Forethought, or Logos) with Salome, which he equates with Eros.[138] Jung's commentary parallels the Logos-Epinoia relationship expounded by Simon Magus, a relationship realized in union with Helena. When Jung scribed his 1920s scrutiny of the encounter with Elijah and Salome, he declared, "They might just as well have been called Simon Magus and Helena."[139]

Jung found an intimate mirror of the tale of Simon and Helena in his observation of the soul. Like Simon, Jung's encounter with the mystery of the soul was apparently opened by love for a woman. On

14 November 1913, Jung addressed his soul: "And I found you again only through the soul of the woman."[140] Throughout *Psychology of the Transference*, and then again in his psychological commentary on "Anima and Animus" in *Aion*—the next volume of his last quartet—Jung avowed that the anima can "be realized only through a relation to a partner of the opposite sex."[141] This complex liaison with the anima played a foundational role in Jung's subjective psychology; Simon's consort, Helena, is often mentioned in his later works. In 1927 he wrote, "The anima-type is presented in the most succinct and pregnant form in the Gnostic legend of Simon Magus."[142]

The Golden Thread

Jung recorded quite a bit about his side of the story. But how did Toni Wolff handle her half? How did a twenty-six year old woman respond to Jung and his vision of their love? Sabina Spielrein's private record offers a glimpse into one woman's earlier experience with Jung, but that liaison was only a shadow of Wolff's encounter. Maybe histories will some day include Toni's own account; Wolff kept a large cache of private journals which may span the period from her adolescent years up until her death. But Wolff was a private woman, and her journals remain guarded in private hands.[143] The dignity and privacy of a human life sometimes trumps historical curiosity; thus, at least for now, Toni Wolff's half of the tale remains mostly a matter of conjecture.

In the "Seven Sermons to the Dead"—Jung's summary revelation in *Liber Novus*, initially recorded in 1916[144]—the differences between male and female experiences of spirituality and sexuality are addressed. The version of the sermons in *Liber Novus* has Philemon speaking the Fifth Sermon, which takes up this subject:

> The world of the Gods is made manifest in spirituality and in sexuality. The celestial ones appear in spirituality, the earthly in sexuality.-...

> Man and woman become devils to each other if they do not separate their spiritual ways, for the essence of creation is differentiation.

> The sexuality of man goes toward the earthly, the sexuality of woman goes toward the spiritual. Man and woman become devils to each other if they do not distinguish their sexuality.

Man shall know the smaller, woman the greater.[145]

Whether or not one judges those statements to be accurate, Jung had evidently observed that men and women encounter sexuality and spirituality from different perspectives. This probably surfaced in his relationship with Toni, and with his wife Emma. Jung had a distinctly introverted nature. His primary interest was the psychic matrix underlying human experience, and Jung was occasionally criticized for not giving adequate interest to his extraverted human relationships.[146] In 1930, Jung related how great poetic creations such as *Shepherd of Hermas*, *The Divine Comedy* and *Faust* all relate "a preliminary love-episode which culminates in a visionary experience. ... We find the undisguised personal love-episode not only connected with the weightier visionary experience but actually subordinated to it."[147] The same seems to have been true of his *Liber Novus*. For Jung, the visionary experience was the weightier issue—it was the essential factor in achieving human "wholeness" and "individuation."

And yet, love magically mediated the task. Jung remarked in a 1916 talk to the Psychological Club that he could either "give my love to the soul," or, as a lover, to "the human being through whom I receive the gift of God." He continued,

> But ... if a man's libido goes to the unconscious, the less it goes to a human being; if it goes to a human being, the less it goes to the unconscious. But if it goes to a human being, and it is a true love, then it is the same as if the libido went direct to the unconscious, so very much is the other person a representative of the unconscious, though only if this other person is truly loved.
>
> Only then does love give him the quality of a mediator, which otherwise and in himself he would not possess.[148]

It was a relational conundrum. If one's partner is "truly loved," then that human being becomes a "representative of the unconscious." Love is a mediator, circulating energy both outwardly and inwardly. Still, projections eventually needed to be taken home to the source. Though a lover might fully represent one's unconscious, the person is in fact a real individual, apart from the magic and *maya* of one's projected images. So, what is left of love when all the projections come home? Jung described the final facts in *Psychology of*

the Transference. What remained he named with distinctly unroman-
tic words: it was "kinship libido."[149] That sounds like a harsh end for
true love. But then, to see a human partner as kin means recognizing
a bond of blood. That can be a profound conjunction, a "higher human relationship." He explained his meaning more poetically to Esther Harding in 1925; he called it then "the Golden Thread":

> Dr. Jung talked about the various forms of relationship, about
> sexuality, about friendship.... There is a third kind of relation-
> ship, the only lasting one, in which it is as though there were
> an invisible telegraph wire between two human beings. He
> said, "I call it, to myself, the Golden Thread." ... It is only
> when the veil of *maya,* of illusion, is rent for us that we can
> begin to recognize the Golden Thread.[150]

In the Protocols, Jung said more to Jaffé about the evolution of
his relationship with Wolff. Speaking of the years he worked on *Liber Novus,* he recalled that he gradually became "conscious," and
met his center. In the measure to which he attained insight, Toni
also found her center. But then, he adds, "she got stuck somewhere
along the way." Jung observed that for Toni, he remained "too much
the center that functioned for her." Toni expected Jung "to be as she
wanted me to be, or that she needed to have me be."[151] Whatever
those private tensions, their relationship continued on varying and
less intimate levels until Toni's death in 1953. And so did his sustaining relationship with Emma.

Barbara Hannah recites another comment made by Jung about
the relationship with Toni during the years of his visionary journey:

> He once told me ... he could never forget what she did for
> him then. He said: "Either she did not love me and was indif-
> ferent concerning my fate, or she loved me—as she certainly
> did—and then it was nothing short of heroism. Such things
> stand forever, and I shall be grateful to her in all eternity."[152]

What was Emma Jung's response to all of this? She was an ex-
tremely private woman, and left few personal remarks in public record. Her surviving letters and private writings have not been
exposed. Emma unquestionably shouldered a socially anomalous
and personally difficult situation. In adult years, Jung's children
were understandably resentful of his relationship with Wolff and its
effect on their family. Nonetheless, throughout her life Emma stood

beside Jung as a companion and wife. Hannah claims that Emma even commented privately to her in later years, "You see, he never took anything from me to give Toni, but the more he gave her, the more he seemed able to give me."[153] Whatever the struggles, I suspect both Emma and Carl recognized their Golden Thread.

IV.

The Psychology of the Transference takes a conceptual tone unlike any of the three following books in Jung's last quartet. Though he is commenting about his observations on the mystery of human relationship and love, Jung abstracts conclusions and parses them within the language of his psychological science. Man and woman, *adept* and *soror mystica*, are couched clinically as patient and doctor. Of course, the transference relationship in analytic therapy did sometimes captivate doctor and patient, and kindle the fires of love. Jung was making valid observations about the nature of the *coniunctio* archetype and the transformative images of union it could arouse in an analytic encounter. However, as he worked on the book, he sensed something was wrong. His approach was amiss, and—as he soon realized—the hermeneutic stumble presaged a nearly fatal fall.

In my first installment to this commentary on the last quartet, "Jung and *Aion:* Time, Vision and a Wayfaring Man," I presented some of this history in greater detail; here I focus on the events in relation to the writing of *The Psychology of the Transference*.[154]

Break a Leg

In February 1944, after completing most of the manuscript for *The Psychology of the Transference,* Jung slipped in the snow and broke his ankle. This modest injury—treated with a too tight cast and complete immobilization—led to development twelve days later of a venous thrombosis and life-threatening pulmonary embolism. For three weeks thereafter, Jung hung between life and death.

And in that twilight of death, he was immersed in a prolonged series of visions. They seemed the end of his journey, the conclusion to the story he had lived. "It is impossible to convey the beauty and intensity of emotion during those visions. They were the most tremendous things I have ever experienced."[155]

I would never have imagined that any such experience was possible. It was not a product of imagination. The visions and experiences were utterly real; there was nothing subjective about them; they all had a quality of absolute objectivity.

We shy away from the word "eternal," but I can describe the experience only as the ecstasy of a non-temporal state in which present, past, and future are one. Everything that happens in time had been brought together into a concrete whole. Nothing was distributed over time, nothing could be measured by temporal concepts.[156]

Before his fall, Jung had been grappling with his initial commentary on the mystical marriage, and reflecting on his experiences with love during the writing of *Liber Novus*. For three decades he had been following the implications of that experience. The path had led him wandering through the visionary traditions of the West searching experiential evidences for a story he knew was not his alone. Jung eventually judged he had identified its thread stretching across centuries, from early Gnostic tradition, through Hermeticism, Alchemy, and Jewish Kabbalah.

Hidden somewhere within all these traditions, he recognized the unifying fact of a central and defining experience. He judged it to be the same imaginative, mythopoetic initiation he had in measure shared—a *mysterium coniunctionis*, historically symbolized in the holy wedding of two natures named with many names: divine and human, male and female, eros and logos, king and queen, salt and sulfur, inner and outer, sense and nonsense, Above and Below. Now his path apparently reached its experiential conclusion. In vision, Jung entered the bridal chamber, and discovered: "I was the marriage." He described the visions:

It was the mystic marriage as it appears in the Cabbalistic tradition. I cannot tell you how wonderful it was. I could only think continually, "Now this is the garden of pomegranates! Now this is the marriage of Malchuth with Tifereth!" I do not know exactly what part I played in it. At bottom it was I myself: I was the marriage. And my beatitude was that of a blissful wedding.

... There followed the Marriage of the Lamb, in a Jerusalem festively bedecked. I cannot describe what it was like in detail.

These were ineffable states of joy. Angels were present, and light. I myself was the "Marriage of the Lamb."

That, too, vanished, and there came a new image, the last vision. I walked up a wide valley to the end, where a gentle chain of hills began. The valley ended in a classical amphitheater. It was magnificently situated in the green landscape. And there, in this theater, the *hierosgamos* was being celebrated.[157]

Barbara Hannah, an observer close to Jung during this period, characterized the illness and visions as being something like a second "rite of initiation"—the first great initiation having been his visionary passage thirty years earlier, recorded in *Liber Novus*. She described these final visions as "the greatest milestone in Jung's attainment of wholeness."[158] Hannah continued, "It most certainly changed and developed Jung to an incalculable extent."[159]

This illness, these visions, and a year of convalescence—followed by a second serious cardiac event in November of 1946—deeply affected Jung's perspective upon his life, his story, and the task remaining to him. They marked the summation of an experience foreshadowed by *Liber Novus*, and gave immediate origin to the next three books of his final quartet.

"At the beginning of the illness," Jung noted, "I had the feeling that there was something wrong with my attitude."[160] Speaking about his approach to the "mystical marriage" in *Psychology of the Transference*, he explained in a private interview:

> The fracture of my fibula was highly symbolic to me. I asked myself for some time where my fault lay. ... After a while I found out: I had trespassed into foreign territory. (It is as if one were walking in one's garden after dark and had fallen into a hole.) ... I had written about anima and animus believing I was just working with psychology; but I had transgressed into "God's country." Alchemy had seemed to me to be a legitimate branch of science but its contents—anima, animus, the self, the alchemical marriage—are not simply scientific concepts; they are gods.[161]

"This Book—My Last"

This second visionary initiation *was* transformative. It refocused Jung on the core experience of his life and on "how important it is to affirm one's own destiny."[162] He recognized that his initial endeavor writing about the *mysterium coniunctionis* in *Psychology of the Transference* was inadequate. It was a prelude to the final opus, but not its consummation.[163] Three more volumes would come, each in turn offering a thematic perspective on conceptions originating with *Liber Novus*.

The work to erupt next after his near-death visions of 1944 was *Aion*—the second addition to the last quartet. Jung explained about *Aion*, which was begun in 1947 and published in 1951:

> Before my illness I had often asked myself if I were permitted to publish or even speak of my secret knowledge. I later set it all down in *Aion*. I realized it was my duty to communicate these thoughts, yet I doubted whether I was allowed to give expression to them. During my illness I received confirmation and I now knew that everything had meaning and that everything was perfect.[164]

After finishing *Aion*, Jung feverishly composed *Answer to Job*. He described this third supplement to his quartet as a continuation of the prior text: "The inner root of this book is to be found in *Aion*."[165] When, in October 1954, he penned a foreword to the fourth and closing volume of the quartet—now finally titled *Mysterium Coniunctionis*—Dr. Jung felt that a duty had been fulfilled. He began the foreword stating it was "my last" book.[166]

Assembled in contemporary reflection, these four books meld as a complex commentary on the creative and imaginative cauldron that produced *Liber Novus*. But, of course, none of Jung's readers in past years could have possibly understood these expositions within this context. Until publication in 2009, *Liber Novus* remained sequestered from public view. And Jung never explicitly indicated the books were a commentary on his unpublished "Red Book." Nonetheless, when they are together summed with source and conception, it is apparent this quartet squares a circular reflection on "the numinous beginning, which contained everything."

Perhaps the strongest evidence I can offer in support of this assertion is a close reading of Dr. Jung himself. In the scope of his life work, it seems inconceivable that C. G. Jung would have declared any book his last book until his New Book had been given final comment. But one is left pondering: Why did Jung think he had stumbled in the formulation of *The Psychology of the Transference*, and why had that misstep nearly kill him? What motivated such dramatic and dire after-thoughts? What subject was of such extraordinary importance that, by a failure in hermeneutic form, he might forfeit his life? The only answer I can find to such strange questions is that in *The Psychology of the Transference* Jung was writing about the most consequential event in his life. He was grasping after language that might convey some understanding of what had happened to him during the years that led to *Liber Novus*. He saw the effort as the consummation of his life's work. To fail was to forfeit. And in this first effort, Jung soon judged that he had fallen short.

After *The Psychology of the Transference*, Jung largely abandoned his scientific and conceptual language. In the following three works, he turned increasingly to the revelatory and soteriological implications of *Liber Novus*. With his next book, *Aion*, he revealed his vision of a coming new age of human consciousness. In *Answer to Job*, which Sonu Shamdasani has called the "theology of *Liber Novus*,"[167] he addressed the transformation of the God image in creaturely incarnation. Finally, in *Mysterium Coniunctionis*, he returned to the function of mythopoetic imagination as agent of that conjunction.

V.

Love was an animating mystery in the life of C. G. Jung. It later became a passage misunderstood, and it cast shadows into the analytic fold that followed after him. Boundary violations within therapeutic relationships were a dark fact too common and too slowly faced by the psychological community following after Jung. One analyst remarked to me years ago that she considered *The Psychology of the Transference* to be nothing but a book for male analytic malpractice. I understood what she meant.

A male analyst who has not yet met his anima will eventually find her in a patient's face. Projected, a bond can form both ways. The mercurial agent of eros may lead one in futile quests "from one bridal chamber to the next."[168] Love is a power that fires the human soul: unmet, unanalyzed, unlived, love seeks physical facts. The "coniunctio neurosis" will sometimes fracture analytic boundaries—as Jung both understood and cautioned. But it can also be the agent to higher human relationships, and sacred unions, if one can only pierce the *maya* of projections, bring home the images, and enter the wedding awaited in the world of the soul. That is, by all evidence, a challenging task. It engages the whole of woman and man.

In *Memories, Dreams, Reflections*, Aniela Jaffé gave this summary of Jung's 1957 comments about sexuality:

> It is a widespread error to imagine that I do not see the value of sexuality. On the contrary, it plays a large part in my psychology as an essential—though not the sole—expression of psychic wholeness. But my main concern has been to investigate, over and above its personal significance and biological function, its spiritual aspect and its numinous meaning, and thus to explain what Freud was so fascinated by but was unable to grasp. My thoughts on this subject are contained in "The Psychology of the Transference" and the *Mysterium Coniunctionis*. Sexuality is of the greatest importance as the expression of the chthonic spirit. That spirit is the "other face of God," the dark side of the God-image.[169]

And then, in the section called "Late Thoughts," Jung offered other final words about Eros, the god so difficult to grasp:

> In classical times, when such things were properly understood, Eros was considered a god whose divinity transcended our human limits, and who therefore could neither be comprehended nor represented in any way. I might, as many before me have attempted to do, venture an approach to this daimon, whose range of activity extends from the endless spaces of the heavens to the dark abysses of hell; but I falter before the task of finding the language which might adequately express the incalculable paradoxes of love. Eros is a *kosmogonos*, a creator and father-mother of all higher consciousness. I sometimes feel that Paul's words—"Though I speak with the tongues of men and of angels, and have not love"—might well be the first condition of all cognition and the quintessence of divinity itself. Whatever the learned interpretation may be of the sentence "God is love," the words affirm the *complexio oppositorum* of the Godhead. In my medical experience as well as in my own life I have again and again been faced with the mystery of love, and have never been able to explain what it is.[170]

But the most poignant of Jung's concluding statements on love was recorded in 1959 by Miguel Serano:

"The process of the mystic wedding involves various stages," Jung explained, "and is open to innumerable risks, like the *Opus Alchemicum*. For this union is in reality a process of mutual individuation...."

Jung went on as though he were talking to himself:

"Somewhere there was once a Flower, a Stone, A Crystal, a Queen, a King, a Palace, a Lover and his Beloved, and this was long ago, on an Island somewhere in the sea five thousand years ago.... Such is Love, the Mystic Flower of the Soul. This is the Center, the Self....

Jung spoke as though he were in a trance. "Nobody understands what I mean;" he said, "only a poet could begin to understand...."[171]

Figure 4
From an 18th century English edition of *Rosarium Philosophorum*.
(MS Ferguson 210, University of Glasgow Library.)

NOTES

I wish to thank Dr. John Peck for his generous editorial assistance. This essay is written in loving memory of my bride and *soror mystica*, Jacquelyn Lemley Owens (1948–2014).

1   "The letters of C. G. Jung to Sabina Spielrein," *Journal of Analytical Psychology*, 2001, 46:177.

2   C. G. Jung, *The Red Book: Liber Novus*, ed. Sonu Shamdasani, tr. John Peck, Mark Kyburz, and Sonu Shamdasani (W.W. Norton & Co, 2009), 264. (Hereafter cited as *Liber Novus*). This work is some-times referenced simply as the "Red Book." A distinction must be made: "The Red Book" is the calligraphic red-leather-bound volume into which Jung eventually transcribed about two-thirds of his draft manuscripts. When speaking hereafter about the "Red Book," I spe-cifically reference the physical folio volume transcribed by Jung. Cita-tions to *Liber Novus* reference the published edition of Jung's manuscripts, above, as edited and compiled by Sonu Shamdasani.

3   *Liber Novus*, 315.

4   Black Book 7, Feb 23, 1920; *Liber Novus*, 307 n240.

5   25 November 1922, *C. G. Jung: Letters*, Gerhard Adler ed. (Princeton: Princeton University Press, 1975), Vol. I, 38-9.

6   C. G. Jung, *Memories, Dreams, Reflections*, Aniela Jaffe´ ed. (Rev. ed., New York: Vintage Books, 1965), 353. (Hereafter cites as MDR.)

7   *Liber Novus*, 317.

8   *Liber Novus*, vii. In MDR the comment is rendered by Aniela Jaffé: "I have never lost touch with my initial experiences. All my works, all my creative activity, has come from those initial fantasies and dreams which began in 1912, almost fifty years ago. Everything that I accom-plished in later life was already contained in them..." MDR, 191.

9   C. G. Jung, *The Black Books of C. G. Jung (1913-1932)*, ed. Sonu Shamdasani, (Stiftung der Werke von C. G. Jung & W. W. Norton & Company), forthcoming. Approximately fifty percent of the text of *The Red Book: Liber Novus* derives directly from the Black Books.

10 Shamdasani, *Liber Novus*, 221.

11 "Tavistock lectures" (1935), C. G. Jung, *Collected Works* (Princeton: Princeton Univ. Press), 18, §275. (Hereafter the *Collected Works* are cited as CW.)

12 Ibid., §277.

13 "On the Nature of the Psyche" (1946), CW 8, §421.

14 *Liber Novus*, 232 n39.

15 *Liber Novus*, 232. In the journal entry, 12 November 1913, the comment begins, "Meine Seele, meine Seele, wo bist Du?"

16 The text given here in italics appears in Black Book 2 but not in the Red Book transcription; *Liber Novus*, 233 n49.

17 Black Book 2, 58; *Liber Novus*, 200 n67.

18 Shamdasani, *Liber Novus*, 199ff.

19 *Liber Novus*, 247 n176.

20 MDR, 189; "It is always only a few who reach the rim of the world, where its mirror-image begins." *Psychological Types*, CW 6, §281.

21 C. G. Jung, *Analytical Psychology: Notes of the Seminar Given in 1925*, William McGuire ed. (Princeton: Princeton University Press, 1989), 34.

22 Sonu Shamdasani, *C. G. Jung: A Biography in Books* (New York: W. W. Norton & Co., 2012), 202.

23 In 1934, Bernhard Baur Celio asked Jung whether he possessed any "secret knowledge" surpassing his written formulations. Jung replied: "I cannot leave your 'question of conscience' unanswered. Obviously I speak only of what I know and what can be verified. ... Beyond that I have had experiences which are, so to speak, 'ineffable' 'secret' because they can never be told properly and because nobody can understand them (I don't know whether I have even approximately understood them myself), 'dangerous' because 99% of humanity would declare I was mad if they heard such things from me, 'catastrophic' because the prejudices aroused by their telling might block other people's way to a living and wondrous mystery, 'taboo' because they are a *numinous precinct* protected by *fear of the Gods*...." 30 January 1934, Letters I, 140-1.   Much later, he spoke about his "secret knowledge" in comments recorded by Margaret Ostrowski-Sachs, *From Conversations with C. G. Jung* (Zürich: Juris Druck & Verlag, 1971), 68.

24 Shamdasani, *Liber Novus*, 202f.

25 "The Psychology of the Transference," published in 1946 (CW 16, 163-323), was largely written prior to the 1944 near-death visions, but published in their reflection. Work on *Aion: Researches into the Phenomenology of the Self* began in 1947; it was published in 1951 (CW 9ii.) *Answer to Job* was first published in 1952 (CW 11, 355-470). *Mysterium Coniunctionis* was completed in 1954 and published in 1955 (CW 14).

26 Shamdasani, *Liber Novus*, 219.

27 Shamdasani, *Biography in Books*, 196n. Shamdasani gives a photograph of the manuscript page.

28 Lance S. Owens, "Jung and *Aion*: Time, Vision and a Wayfaring Man;" *Psychological Perspectives* (Journal of the C. G. Jung Institute of Los Angeles, 2011) 54:253-89. (Online edition available.)

29 MDR, 181-3.

30 *Liber Novus*, 245-6.

31 *Liber Novus*, 250 n197.

32 *Liber Novus*, 356. This commentary was probably written in the early 1920s, it is given as Appendix B in *Liber Novus*.

33 *Liber Novus*, 252.

34 *Liber Novus*, 356.

35 *Liber Novus*, 255 n240. The English edition of *Liber Novus* uniformly employs the word "pleasure" to translate "die Lust;" the word might more meaningfully be translated as "desire" or "desiring." In German, "die Lust" implies joy, appetite, lust, pleasure, desire, inclination, or all of these combined. The meaning includes an aspect of instinctual and fleshly desire that can be sexual. Jung indicates this translation: "pleasure [*die Lust*] is the force that desires and destroys forms without form and definition." *Liber Novus*, 247.

36 *Liber Novus*, 254 n238.

37 *Liber Novus*, 255 n240; translation modified, *die Lust* is translated here as "desire" or "desiring."

38 Portions of this text were lined out in the draft; *Liber Novus*, 255 n240.

39 *Liber Novus*, Appendix B, 365ff.

40 "Logos undoubtedly has the upper hand in this, my case, since Elijah says that he and his daughter have always been one. Yet Logos and Eros are not one, but two. In this case, however, Logos has blinded and subjugated Eros." *Liber Novus*, Appendix B, 366.

41 *Liber Novus*, 250 n197.

42 "Such primordial images have a secret power that works just as much on human reason as on the soul. Wherever they appear they stir something linked with the mysterious, the long gone, and heavy with foreboding. A string sounds whose vibration reverberates in every man's breast; these primordial images dwell in everyone as they are the property of all mankind. This secret power is like a spell, like magic,

and causes elevation just as much as seduction. It is characteristic of primordial images that they take hold of man where he is utterly human, and a power seizes him, as if the bustling throng were pushing him. And this happens even if individual understanding and feeling rise up against it. What is the power of the individual against the voice of the whole people in him? He is entranced, possessed, and consumed. Nothing makes this effect clearer than the serpent. It signifies everything dangerous and everything bad, everything nocturnal and uncanny, which adheres to Logos as well as to Eros, so long as they can work as the dark and unrecognized principles of the unconscious spirit." *Liber Novus*, Appendix B, 365.

43   *Liber Novus*, Appendix B, 366.

44   9 April 1959, Letters I, 19 n8.

45   "[Freud] was fascinated by the dark side of Man, i.e. by all those things, that make out the contents of the 'Mysterium Iniquitatis', the mystery of the shadow. Without his emphasis on the dark side of Man and the chaos of his chthonic desires, I could not have found an access to the 'Mysterium Coniunctionis'." Letter to R. F. C. Hull, 27 December 1958, Carl G. Jung Protocols Collection, Library of Congress (LOC). At the time of this letter, Hull was translating *Mysterium Coniunctionis*.

46   The unusual compound Greek word ἐναντιοδρομίας occurs in a summary of the philosophy of Heraclitus by Diogenes Laërtius, c. 3rd century CE. Jung seems to have coined its meaning in modern usage.

47   Compare the Prophet Elijah as a representative of "otherworldly" images.

48   Compare Salome ascending from the darkness.

49   "The Spirit of Mercurius," CW 13, §294.

50   In his October 1954 preface to *Mysterium Coniunctionis*, Jung attributes the books origin as follows: "This book—my last—was begun more than ten years ago. I first got the idea of writing it from C. Kerényi's essay on the Aegean Festival in Goethe's *Faust*. The literary prototype of this festival is *The Chymical Wedding* of Christian Rosencreutz, itself a product of the traditional hierosgamos symbolism of alchemy." Foreword to *Mysterium Coniunctionis*, CW 14, p. xiii. In 1971 Aniela Jaffé also affirmed that Kerényi's essay stimulated Jung's work; Aniela Jaffé, "Phases in Jung's Life," *Spring: An Annual of Archetypal Psychology and Jungian Thought* (New York: Spring Publications, 1972), 182-3.

51   8 August 1951, cited in Shamdasani, *Biography in Books*, 196.

52 Ibid.; these first lines were later crossed out in the manuscript.

53 Ibid.

54 The manuscript was completed in autumn 1945, and initially published as: *Die Psychologie der Ubertragung. Erläutert anhand einer alchemistischen Bilderserie für Ärzte und praktische Psychologen* (Zürich: Rascher, 1946). The subtitle, "Explained on the basis of a series alchemical images for physicians and practical psychologists," appears only in the original edition; "The Psychology of the Transference," CW 16, 164-323. (Hereafter cited as Psych. Transference.)

55 "The important part played ... by the *coniunctio*, corresponds to the central significance of the transference in psychotherapy on the one hand and in the field of normal human relationships on the other." Ibid., §538.

56 This and following paragraph references are to "The Psychology of the Transference," CW 16.

57 In Latin, *concupiscentia* implies "longing, desire." Ibid., §361

58 See also, "On the Nature of the Psyche" (1946), CW 8, §415ff.

59 Jung had the initial 1550 edition in his library, *Rosarium Philosophorum* (Frankfurt: C. Jacob, 1550); this work appeared in at least fifteen other late-sixteenth century alchemical manuscripts. In the various editions, the treatise usually contained 20 woodcuts; Jung selected an initial series of eleven for use in his commentary.

60 Psych. Transference, §422ff.

61 Ibid., §398.

62 "The sexuality of the unconscious was instantly taken with great seriousness and elevated to a sort of religious dogma, which has been fanatically defended right down to the present time: such was the fascination emanating from those contents which had last been nurtured by the alchemists. The natural archetypes that underlie the mythologems of incest, the hierosgamos, the divine child, etc., blossomed forth—in the age of science—into the theory of infantile sexuality, perversions, and incest, while the *coniunctio* was rediscovered in the transference neurosis." Ibid., §533

63 *Liber Novus*, 264.

64 Portions of this text were lined out in the draft; see *Liber Novus*, 255 n240; *Corrected Draft*, 150.

65 On Jung's early relationship with Emma, an embellished outline appears in Deirdre Bair, *Jung: A Biography* (New York: Little, Brown and Co., 2003), 70-83.

66 For a sympathetic remembrance of Emma Jung, which emphasizes the difficulties of her situation, see: Imelda Guaadissart, *Love and Sacrifice: The Life of Emma Jung*, tr. Kathleen Llanwarne (Asheville: Chiron, 2014). This book unfortunately includes several historical misstatements and provides scant references to sources.

67 Psych. Transference, §503.

68 Psych. Transference, §362-3

69 Zvi Lothane, "Tender love and transference: Unpublished letters of C. G. Jung and Sabina Spielrein," in C. Covington and B. Wharton, eds., *Sabina Spielrein: Forgotten Pioneer of Psychoanalysis* (Hove: Brunner-Routledge, 2003), 189-222.

70 Ibid., 221.

71 Ibid., 203; translated from Russian by Lothane, emphasis in the original. A differently edited version of the letter is given by Lothane, *International Journal of Psychoanalysis*, 80 (1999), 1189–1204.

72 Aldo Carotenuto, *A Secret Symmetry: Sabina Spielrein Between Jung and Freud* (New York: Pantheon Books, 1982), 13.

73 Four years later Jung wrote in *Liber Novus*, "I must catch up with a piece of the Middle Ages—within myself. We have only finished the Middle Ages of—others." *Liber Novus*, 330.

74 "Unedited extracts from a diary," *Journal of Analytical Psychology*, 46, 1, 157.

75 Ibid., 162. Spielrein continues, "one loves one's ideal in the other; a short separation strengthens love because one prefers to remember the ideal image. But the ideal is nothing other than that which is deeply anchored in the psyche as a result of an infinity of circumstances."

76 Ibid., 168.

77 Psych. Transference, §469.

78 This would have been his initial journal, "Black Book 1"; Jung stopped writing in this journal around the time of his marriage in 1903.

79 "Unedited extracts from a diary," *Journal of Analytical Psychology*, 46:1, 169.

80 Ibid., 156.

81 Ibid., 163.

82 "The Letters of C. G. Jung to Sabina Spielrein," *Sabina Spielrein: Forgotten Pioneer of Psychoanalysis*, 57; a less accurate translation of this passage is given in John Kerr, *A Most Dangerous Method* (New York: Alfred A. Knopf, 1993), 491.

83 Lothane, *Sabina Spielrein: Forgotten Pioneer of Psychoanalysis*, 203-4. Emma Jung wrote Freud, "Naturally the women are all in love with him..." 24 November 1911, William McGuire, ed., *The Freud/Jung Letters* (Princeton: Princeton University Press, 1974), 465.

84 11 February 1910, Letters I, 17-18.

85 *Liber Novus*, 272.

86 Freud to Ferenczi, 23 December 1912, *The Correspondence of Sigmund Freud and Sándor Ferenczi, Volume 1, 1908–1914*, 446; see also, Shamdasani, *Cult Fictions: C. G. Jung and the Founding of Analytical Psychology*. (London: Routledge, 1998), 57. Shamdasani notes, "Jung's pupil Jolande Jacobi recalled, 'I heard from others, about the time before he [Jung] met Toni Wolff, that he had a love affair there in the Burghölzli with a girl—what was her name? Moltzer'." 57 n3. Jung's claimed "analysis" might be attributed in some part to Dr. Spielrein.

87 Sonu Shamdasani, "The lost contributions of Maria Moltzer to analytical psychology: two unknown papers," *Spring: Journal of Archetype and Culture* 64 (1998), 103–120.

88 In the Protocols, Jung states he knew Moltzer from 1912 to 1918, however the association started at least two years earlier; Moltzer is mentioned in a letter to Freud (8 September 1910, *Freud/Jung Letters*, 351), and was a member of the Zürich contingent attending the Weimar Congress in 1911. During his October 1912 visit to New York, Jung presented one of Moltzer's cases; a month later Moltzer followed Jung to New York, and lodged with Dr. Beatrice Hinkle (U. S. Immigration Records). Hinkle would shortly thereafter translate into English Jung's 1912 work, *Wandlungen und Symbole der Libido* (*Psychology of the Unconscious*, CW B). In 1915, Jung described his professional relationship with Moltzer to the New York physician Smith Ely Jelliffe, "I only can tell you how I behaved in the case of my assistant [Moltzer]: I trusted the cases entirely to her with the only condition, that in case of difficulties she would consult me or send the patient to me in order to be controlled by myself. But this arrangement existed in the beginning only. Later on Miss M. worked quite independently and quite efficiently. ... I arranged weekly meetings with my assistant, where everything was settled carefully and on an analytical basis." Jung to Jelliffe, late-July 1915, John C. Burnham and William McGuire, *Jelliffe: American Psychoanalyst and Physician and His Correspondence with Sigmund Freud and C. G. Jung*, 198. Also see Shamdasani, *Cult Fictions*, 57. All references to the Protocols are to the X. Roelli typescript translation prepared for William McGuire in

1979; Carl G. Jung Protocols, Box 1, Library of Congress. (Hereafter cited as Roelli typescript, Protocols.)

89 Jung talked with Jaffé about Moltzer: "I had a Dutch patient, a woman, a terrific creature who had an enormous transference to me. Through her the anima dawned on me. In the beginning, when I wrote these things there was this voice whispering to me 'this is art', and that was her voice." Roelli typescript, p. 31, Protocols. Moltzer was at that time the only Dutch patient in his circle; see Shamdasani, *Cult Fictions*.

90 This is most apparent in Moltzer's 1917 papers; see *Cult Fictions*, Appendix I and II, 85-105. For indications of the dialogue, compare these talks by Moltzer with Jung's October 1916 talk, "Adaptation, Individuation, Collectivity," CW 18, §1084-1106.

91 Shamdasani, *Liber Novus*, 203-6.

92 "The air began to clear when I dropped the Dutch patient who was trying to suggest to me that what I was making was art...." Roelli typescript, p. 32, LOC.

93 Roelli typescript p. 31, Protocols.

94 "Confrontation with the Unconscious," Chapter 6 in MDR, 170ff.

95 On the construction of MDR, see Sonu Shamdasani, "Memories, Dreams, Omissions," *Spring: Journal of Archetype and Culture*, 1995, 115 – 137, reprinted in Barry Bishop ed., *Jung in Contexts*, (London: Routledge, 1999), 33-50.

96 Following publication of Jung's Black Book journals, Jaffé's stenographic transcript of Jung's personal recollections, recorded in 1957, remains the most important primary archival source on Jung still begging publication.

97 Barbara Hannah arrived in Zürich in 1929; over the following decades she associated closely with Jung, his wife Emma, and Toni Wolff. She heard a good deal about Jung's life from first-hand accounts. Barbara Hannah, *Jung: His Life and Work* (New York: G. Putnam's Sons, 1976).

98 Jung to Freud, 29 August 1911. *Freud/Jung Letters*, 440.

99 These statements in the Protocols were first summarized by Sonu Shamdasani, "Memories, Dreams, Omissions," *Jung in Contexts*, 40f.; Roelli typescript, Protocols.

100 MDR, 171.

101 Black Book Journal 2, p. 17; cited in Shamdasani, *Liber Novus*, 198.

102 Psych. Transference, §378.

103 Ibid., §471.

104 *Analytical Psychology*, 42; Shamdasani, *Liber Novus*, 199.

105 Hannah, 124.

106 "I was much interested in the fact that a woman should interfere with me from within. My conclusion was that it must be the soul in primitive sense, and I began to speculate on the reasons that the name "anima" was given to soul. ... From the trouble it took me to put up with the interference I had from the anima figure, I could measure the power of the unconscious, and it was great indeed." *Analytical Psychology*, 44-5.

107 Deirdre Bair was adept at creating fictitious scenes in her biography of Jung; for example, this description of private conversations between Jung and Wolff: "Usually he paced and talked as Toni hunched forward listening intently. She interrupted often, and he used the pauses to tamp fresh tobacco in his ubiquitous pipe as she gave her interpretations of his visions...." Bair, 249.

108 Psych. Transference, §454, n16.

109 Maria Helena Mandacaru Guerra, *The Love Drama of C. G. Jung: As Revealed in His Life and in His Red Book* (Inner City Books, 2014); first edition in Portuguese, *O Livro Vermelho - O Drama de Amor de C. G. Jung* (Linear B, 2012).

110 Psych. Transference, §448.

111 30 December 1913, Black Book 3; *Liber Novus*, 267 n44.

112 *Liber Novus*, 250 n197.

113 *Liber Novus*, 295

114 Jung was working on his concepts of psychological types throughout this period; see John Beebe and Ernst Falzeder, eds., *The Question of Psychological Types: The Correspondence of C. G. Jung and Hans Schmid-Guisan, 1915-1966* (Princeton: Princeton Univ. Press, 2013).

115 *Liber Novus*, 294, 296.

116 *Liber Novus*, 260.

117 *Liber Novus*, 262-3.

118 *Liber Novus*, 269.

119 *Liber Novus*, 275 n80.

120 *Liber Novus*, 317-8.

121 *Liber Novus*, 356.

122 "From Esther Harding's Notebooks," William McGuire & R.F.C. Hull, eds., *C. G. Jung Speaking: Interviews and Encounters* (Princeton, NJ: Princeton University Press, 1977), 28-9.

123 Psych. Transference, §471.

124 MDR, 183.

125 *Liber Novus*, 315.

126 See Jung's 1917 comparison of Goethe and Nietzsche, C. G. Jung, *Collected Papers on Analytical Psychology* (New York: Moffat Yard and Co., 1917), 383–4.

127 "In the legend of Simon, however, and in the second part of *Faust* anima symbols of complete maturity are found." "Mind and Earth," CW 10, §75-6.

128 *Liber Novus*, 356; on Jung's search for mythic roots, see the Foreword to *Symbols of Transformation*, CW 5, xxv.

129 Hannah, 114; emphasis in the original. The lost writings of Hippolytus were rediscovered in 1852 at the Mt. Athos monastery in Greece. A first Latin edition of Hippolytus appeared in 1859 and this was the edition commonly cited for the next fifty years: L. Duncker & F. G. Schneidewin, ed., *Refutatio Omnium Hæresium* (Göttingen, 1859). The first critical edition in German is: P. Wendland, *Hippolytus Werke III. Refutatio omnium haeresium* (Leipzig, 1916); Jung acquired this edition after 1916 and cited it often in his later works. The first critical English edition is: F. Legge, ed.; *Philosophumena or the Refutation of all Heresies* (London: Soc. for Promoting Christian Knowledge, 1921), and this volume is generally quoted in the English edition of Jung's *Collected Works*.

130 Lance S. Owens, "Foreword," in, Alfred Ribi, *The Search for Roots: C. G. Jung and the Tradition of Gnosis* (Los Angeles: Gnosis Archive Books, 2013), 14-27. (Online edition available.)

131 *Liber Novus*, 359 & n162.

132 Irenaeus, *Contra Haereses*, I. xxiii. 1-4.

133 In Greek, the word ἐπίνοια (epinoia) has feminine gender and implies both "what is on the mind" and "were it leads;" thus, the fact of thought and the result of conceiving thought.

134 Irenaeus, *Contra Haereses*, I. xxiii. 2: "He took round with him a certain Helen, a hired prostitute from the Phoenician city Tyre, after he had purchased her freedom, saying that she was the first conception (or Thought) of his Mind, the Mother of All, by whom in the beginning he conceived in his Mind the making of the Angels and Archan-

gels. That this Thought, leaping forth from him, and knowing what was the will of her Father, descended to the lower regions and generated the Angels and Powers, by whom also he said this world was made. And after she had generated them, she was detained by them through envy, for they did not wish to be thought to be the progeny of any other. As for himself, he was entirely unknown by them; and it was his Thought that was made prisoner by the Powers and Angels that has been emanated by her. And she suffered every kind of indignity at their hands, to prevent her reascending to her Father, even to being imprisoned in the human body and transmigrating into other female bodies, as from one vessel into another."

135 G. R. S. Mead, *Fragments of a Faith Forgotten* (London: Theosophical Publishing Society, 1900, reprint 1906), 168. Jung essentially quotes Mead on this point (without citation) in *Mysterium Coniunctionis*, where Jung states the text "describes a *coniunctio Solis et Lunae*." CW 14, 136.

136 *Liber Novus*, 236.

137 *Liber Novus*, 248.

138 *Liber Novus*, 248; 251 n201; 254 n238. Much later he explained that, "By Logos I meant discrimination, judgment, insight, and by Eros I meant the placing into relation." *Mysterium Coniunctionis*, CW 14, §224.

139 *Liber Novus*, 368.

140 *Liber Novus*, 233 n49.

141 *Aion*, CW 9ii, §42.

142 "Mind and Earth," CW 10, §75-6. In *Mysterium Coniunctionis* Jung speaks of the alchemical workers, "who in the symbolical realm are Sol and Luna, in the human the adept and his soror mystica, and in the psychological realm the masculine consciousness and feminine unconscious (anima)." He notes first among the classic examples of this, "Simon Magus and Helen." CW 14, 153 and n317.

143 Private communication.

144 It appears the Seven Sermons are recorded in journal entries at the end of Black Book 5 and the beginning of Black Book 6, dated 31 January to 8 February 1916. *Liber Novus*, 346 n77; 354 n121.

145 *Liber Novus*, 352.

146 Hans Schmid wrote Jung in December 1915, "There you are, sitting in a tower on the *Obersee* having become Nietzsche's heir, father to none, friend to none, and sufficient unto yourself. Vis-a-vis, here and

there, a few other male and female introverts are living, each in their tower, loving humankind in those 'farthest away,' thus protecting themselves against the devilish love of their closest 'neighbors.' And, from time to time, they meet in the middle of the lake, each in their motorboat, and prove to each other the dignity of man." *The Question of Psychological Types*, 154. This letter was written eight years before Jung would commence building his Tower at Bollingen on the *Obersee*, the southern portion of Lake Zürich.

147 "Psychology and Literature," CW 15, §148.

148 "Adaptation, Individuation, Collectivity," CW 18, §1105-6.

149 Psych. Transference, §445.

150 13 May 1925, "From Esther Harding's Notebooks," 46.

151 Roelli typescript, p. 34, Protocols.

152 Hannah, 120.

153 Ibid., 119-20.

154 Lance S. Owens, "Jung and *Aion*: Time, Vision and a Wayfaring Man," *Psychological Perspectives* (Journal of the C. G. Jung Institute of Los Angeles, 2011) 54:253-89. (Online edition available.)

155 MDR, 295ff. Also see Hannah, 277ff.

156 MDR, 295-6.

157 Ibid., 294.

158 Hannah, 276.

159 Ibid., 282.

160 MDR, 297.

161 Margaret Ostrowski-Sachs, *From Conversations with C. G. Jung* (Zürich : Juris Druck & Verlag, 1971), 68.

162 MDR, 297.

163 Speaking of his work during the prior two years, Jung said after the last visions, "All I have written is correct. ... I only realize its full reality now." Hannah, 279.

164 Ostrowski-Sachs, 68.

165 MDR, 216.

166 *Mysterium Coniunctionis*, CW 14, xiii.

167 Sonu Shamdasani, "Foreword to the 2010 Edition," *Answer to Job* (Princeton: Princeton University Press; Reprint edition, 2010), ix.

168 Psych. Transference, §503.

169 MDR, 168.

170 Ibid., 353.

171 5 May 1959 interview, text slightly modified; Miguel Serrano, *C. G. Jung and Herman Hesse: A Record of Two Friendships* (London: Routledge & Kegan Paul, 1966), 60. Spanish edition, *El Cirulo Hermetico* (Buenos Aires: Kier, 2007), 94-5.

Jung in Love – The *Mysterium* in *Liber Novus*
was originally published in:

Thomas Arzt (Hrsg.)

Das Rote Buch
C. G. Jungs Reise zum
„anderen Pol der Welt"
Studien zur Analytischen Psychologie Band 5
Editorial Board: Friedrich Gaede und Bruno Müller-Oerlinghausen

Überraschend für die Öffentlichkeit wurde im Herbst 2009 ein in seiner Ausstattung prachtvoll konzipiertes Buch veröffentlicht, das seitdem als geistesgeschichtliche Sensation eingeordnet wird und dessen Wirkungen heute wie auch für die Zukunft noch kaum absehbar sind: das *Rote Buch: Liber Novus* von C. G. Jung. Zunächst in einer ersten Auflage von 5.000 Exemplaren veröffentlicht, ist die weltweite Resonanz zum *Roten Buch* mit bis heute mehr als 100.000 verkauften Exemplaren unerwartet groß gewesen.

In den Jahren 1913 bis 1918 hatte sich Jung bei seiner „Nachtmeerfahrt" auf die Suche nach seinem „persönlichen Mythos" begeben. Adressiert an Leser in einer fernen Zukunft ist das *Rote Buch* das schriftliche Zeugnis dieser Suche, bei der Jung nicht nur seinen individuellen Mythos fand, sondern auch Hinweise auf einen neuen, kollektiven Mythos und einen epochalen Wendepunkt der menschlichen Bewusstseinsentwicklung, auf ein kommendes Äon. Jungs „Weg des Kommenden" deutet auf einen Gestaltwandel unseres Gottesbildes hin, der sich heute wohl vollzieht. Das Werk Jungs wird durch die Publikation des *Roten Buches* eine komplette Neuinterpretation erfahren; schon heute wird bei der Lektüre deutlich, in welchem Sinne Jung ein Visionär war und seine Erfahrungen auch etwas Prophetisches haben. Insofern er schreibt, dass der „Geist der Tiefe", den er in seinem Dialog mit dem Unbewussten persönlich erfahren und im *Roten Buch* beschrieben hat, auch gleichzeitig der „Herr der Tiefe des Weltgeschehens" ist, so gehen uns Heutigen diese Erfahrungen stark an in dem Sinne, dass sie uns möglicherweise Hilfe und Navigation in den globalen Transformationsprozessen unserer Zeit zu geben vermögen.

ca. 210 Seiten
Broschur mit Fadenheftung
Format 15,5 x 23,5 cm
Subskriptionspreis € 18,00
(bis 31.03.2015)
ISBN 978-3-8260-5678-9
späterer Ladenpreis ca. € 28,00

Thomas Arzt (Hrsg.)
Das Rote Buch
C. G. Jungs Reise zum „anderen Pol der Welt"
Studien zur Analytischen Psychologie Band 5
K&N

Verlag Königshausen & Neumann GmbH

With Contributions From:

T. Arzt: "Der Weg des Kommenden": C. G. Jungs *Rotes Buch* und seine *Ecclesia Spiritualis* – *H. Weyerstrass*: Das *Rote Buch* als Weg-Eröffner – *W. Schwery*: Die Bedeutung des Mandalas im *Roten Buch* – *T. Cheetham*: To Live in Growing Orbits. The Escape from Subjectivity in Jung, Corbin & Hillman – *H.-J. Koch*: Die Idee der Zwischenwelt bei C. G. Jung und Henry Corbin sowie ihre Bedeutung für die heutige Zeit – *S. Mahmoud*: Henry Corbin and Jung's Visionary Recital: A Preliminary Approach to *The Red Book* – *G. Sauer*: Das Unbewußte als Gesprächpartner für Heute: Angeregt durch das *Rote Buch* – *J. Woodcock*: The Hidden Legacy of *The Red Book* – *A. Holm*: Subjekt versus Kollektiv: Neubestimmung mit dem *Roten Buch* – *L. Owens*: Jung in Love: The *Mysterium* in *Liber Novus*.

Made in United States
Troutdale, OR
11/25/2023

14924484R00046